Lucius Clarke Davis

The Story of the Memorial Foundation to Shakspeare

At Stratford-Upon-Avon

Lucius Clarke Davis

The Story of the Memorial Foundation to Shakspeare
At Stratford-Upon-Avon

ISBN/EAN: 9783337055912

Printed in Europe, USA, Canada, Australia, Japan

Cover: Foto ©ninafisch / pixelio.de

More available books at **www.hansebooks.com**

THE STORY OF

THE MEMORIAL FOUNTAIN TO SHAKSPEARE

AT STRATFORD-UPON-AVON

Honest water that ne'er
left any man in the mire

ALSO ACCOUNTS *OF THE HERBERT* AND COWPER WINDOW,
WESTMINSTER *ABBEY;* THE MILTON WINDOW, ST.
MARGARET'S *CHURCH,* WESTMINSTER; AND THE
BISHOPS ANDRE*WES AND* KEN REREDOS, ST.
THOMAS'*S* CHURCH; WINCHESTER,
ENGLAND — GIFTS OF
GEO. W. CHILDS

EDITED BY
L. CLARKE DAVIS

CAMBRIDGE
Printed at the Riverside Press
1890

EXPLANATORY.

AS there is nothing, however remote or insignificant, connected with SHAKSPEARE that is without value to those who, with BEN JONSON, "love the man," or "do reverence his memory," I have thought that the "story" of The Memorial Fountain erected at Stratford-upon-Avon by Mr. GEORGE W. CHILDS would be neither valueless nor uninteresting.

For the compiling of this Story of the Stratford Fountain, which is but a gathering and putting together of what has been elsewhere said and written, I have no better warrant than that, not only have I found therein a pleasant occupation for some leisure hours, but to me the subject seemed worthy of being revived from the newspapers—in which, through patient delving, I mainly found it—and of receiving a more permanent form.

Explanatory.

Whatever value this book may have lies, I know, solely in the fact that it tells, with more or less completeness, the Story of the Origin, Building, and Dedication of the most imposing architectural monument erected in any country to the genius of SHAKSPEARE. There must be both pride and pleasure to every American in the reflection that this Stratford Memorial is the gift of a fellow-citizen who in giving and building neither gave unwittingly, nor builded better than he knew; he did both in the confident hope and faith, I am convinced, that his gift would add another link—however slight—to that chain of brotherhood between Englishmen and Americans which so many of the leading minds in Religion, in Politics, in Literature, and on the Stage on either side of the Atlantic, have been, during late years, so earnestly engaged in welding firmer, and closer, and stronger.

In selecting that which is herein presented from the great mass of material in the public journals of the day, both English and American, I rejected all that did not seem pertinent to the objects I had in view, whereof the first is to give permanency to the history of the Stratford Fountain, and whereof the other is to let the story bear record of the general recognition of the fine motive which inspired the gift. If I have retained anything which may not seem germane to these objects, and which should, perhaps, have been rejected, I have erred only through a zealous wish to present as much evidence as possible of the sincerity and universality of that international spirit of fraternity to the existence of which the newspapers of the Old Country and of the New testified so strongly in their remarks upon MR. CHILDS'S SHAKSPEARE MEMORIAL.

To the Story of the Fountain I have deemed it not inappropriate to add brief accounts of certain other gifts which, in the interest of the same broad spirit of international brotherhood, Mr. CHILDS, as a representative American, has presented, at different times, to England and to the English people.

L. C. D.

TABLE OF CONTENTS.

	PAGE
I. THE STORY OF THE MEMORIAL FOUNTAIN TO SHAKSPEARE, AT STRATFORD-UPON-AVON	3
II. AN ACCOUNT OF THE WINDOW IN WESTMINSTER ABBEY TO THE MEMORY OF THE CHRISTIAN POETS, HERBERT AND COWPER	159
III. THE WINDOW IN ST. MARGARET'S CHURCH, WESTMINSTER, COMMEMORATIVE OF THE GENIUS OF THE POET MILTON	181
IV. THE MEMORIAL REREDOS ERECTED IN ST. THOMAS'S CHURCH, WINCHESTER, ENGLAND, TO THE PIOUS AND LEARNED BISHOPS ANDREWES AND KEN	239

SHAKESPEARE FOUNTAIN

STRATFORD-UPON-AVON

THE STRATFORD-UPON-AVON FOUNTAIN.

INTRODUCTORY.

THE late J. O. Hallowell-Phillipps begins his 'Outlines of the Life of Shakspeare' in the words following: "In the reign of King Edward the Sixth there lived in Warwickshire a farmer named Richard Shakspeare, who rented a cottage and a small quantity of land at Snitterfield, an obscure village in that county. He had two sons, one of whom, named Henry, continued throughout his life to reside in the same parish. John, the other son, left his father's home about the year 1551, and shortly afterwards is found residing in the neighboring and comparatively large borough of Stratford-upon-Avon."

This John Shakspeare was the father of William Shakspeare, England's and the world's greatest poet, sage, and philosopher, whom Garrick apostrophized as—

> "That demi-god!
> Who Avon's flowery margin trod,
>   While sportive fancy round him flew;
> Where Nature led him by the hand,
>   Instructed him in all she knew,
> And gave him absolute command."

From the days of Ben Jonson, who declared his love for Shakspeare to be as great as that of any, "this side idolatry," to the present time, there has been no lack of pæans chanted to him. But it is one of the most remarkable things concerning the general love and admiration for him that throughout England there was not for centuries after his death a single monument of imposing character erected to his memory.

The poet that filled the spacious times of great Elizabeth with the splendor of his genius, who created a new literature in Germany, who gave original vitality to that of France, and whose work will survive the "wreck of matter and the crush of worlds," had erected to him, by his widow or son-in-law, seven years after his death, in 1623, the rude effigy in Trinity Church at Stratford-upon-Avon; and in 1740 the bust in Westminster Abbey was set up as a memorial of him. There was no other monument subsequently erected, in all England, to Shakspeare until Baron Grant put in Leicester Square the statue which is still there, to serve as a token of a private citizen's public spirit.

In Basse's 'Elegy on Shakspeare,' published in 1633, occur the following lines addressed to the triumvirate of great dead poets lying together in the Poet's Corner in Westminster Abbey:—

> "Renowned Spenser, lie a thought more nigh
> To learned Chaucer; and rare Beaumont, lie
> A little nearer Spenser, to make room
> For Shakspeare in your threefold-fourfold tomb."

To which "rare Ben Jonson" replied:—

> "My Shakspeare, rise; I will not lodge thee by
> Chaucer or Spenser, or bid Beaumont lie
> A little farther off to make thee room.
> Thou art a monument without a tomb,
> And art alive still while thy book doth live,
> And we have wits to read, and praise to give."

Shakspeare's bones still lie undisturbed in the church at Stratford-upon-Avon, and only that poor bust proclaims his presence in the British Pantheon. The reason for this apparent neglect on the part of Englishmen to honor by some form of outward show the fame of the greatest of all poets may possibly be found in the reply of Jonson. He would have no memorial of him erected in the Abbey, as his 'book' was the best and most appropriate monument he could have so long as man had wit to read or praise to give. That thought may have been a common one in the English mind, and, therefore, his loyal countrymen would have no memorial of him which, whatsoever it might be, would still be less than that of the poet's genius, which was his own best monument.

But, however that may be, it is certain that in the Jubilee Year of the Victorian reign, when the Fountain erected at Stratford-upon-Avon by the munificent and catholic spirit of an American citizen was unveiled, it was not only the most imposing monument in all England to Shakspeare, but it was the only one the dignity of which impressed the spectator as in any way worthy to commemorate the genius of that mighty intellectual monarch whose mind was as a throne before which all the world of thought still delights to reverently bow down.

THE INCEPTION OF THE MEMORIAL.

In the autumn of 1878 the Very Reverend Arthur P. Stanley, D.D., Dean of Westminster, visited the United States, and during his sojourn in Philadelphia was, as so many distinguished foreigners previously were and have since been, the guest of MR. GEORGE W. CHILDS. In the course of an after-dinner talk the venerable Dean, whose love of the literature of his country was not less sincere than his knowledge of it was profound, spoke feelingly of the absence of any suitable memorial of some of those who had laid so broad and deep the foundations of English poetry. Especially he spoke of Shakspeare, and of the strange neglect of the British-speaking people to erect an appropriate monument to him even in the place of his birth. The Dean of Westminster was greatly impressed by what he had seen and heard in America, and particularly was he moved by the noble hospitality of which he was everywhere the recipient, and which he was modestly pleased to think emanated not so much from personal regard for himself as from the common feeling of kinship which he felt bound the peoples of the two countries together. For his cousins across the sea he was inspired with admiration, respect, and affection, and his broad and generous sympathies induced him to think that no better thing could be done by Englishmen or Americans than to strengthen the belief that was surely growing up among their leaders of thought in the reality of their mutual feeling of fraternity and fellowship.

The gift of Mr. Childs of the Herbert and Cowper Window to Westminster Abbey had been suggested by Dean Stanley, and it was on the occasion to which reference is above made that this eminent divine ventured to state to his host that a memorial of similar or other character of Shakspeare set up in the Church at Stratford-upon-Avon by an American would have a certain influence for good throughout England and America. Subsequently, after the Dean's return to his own country, Mr. Childs wrote to him to say that he had considered the suggestion of placing a memorial window to Shakspeare in the Church by the Avon, which is the Poet's tomb, and that he would be pleased to make the gift upon the sole condition that Dean Stanley would himself not only determine what form it should assume, but personally undertake the execution of the donor's purpose.

In a letter dated December 3, 1878, Dean Stanley said, in reply to Mr. Childs, "With regard to your generous offer of the window, will you let me delay my complete answer till the week after next, when I shall hope to have seen the Church? I am inclined to think that Stratford being, next to Westminster Abbey, the place (I believe) most frequently visited by Americans, might be considered an exceptional locality."

Subsequently, on December 18, 1878, Dean Stanley wrote, from Stratford-upon-Avon, the subjoined letter:—

"My Dear Mr. Childs:—

"In pursuance of my promise I have come here to look at the Church and see what place there would be for the window which, in accordance with my suggestion, you so kindly offered to give.

"I find that on one side of the chancel there is a place for windows containing subjects from the Old Testament, of which one has already been erected by the collective contributions of Americans, and two others remain to be supplied. It would, I think, be very suitable that the one next in order should come from Philadelphia. It consists of seven or eight compartments, and I would suggest that as the window alongside contains The Seven Ages of Man, taken from different characters of the Old Testament, so the next should contain some other Shakspearian subject also taken from the Old Testament. If you will allow me to think over this, I will do my best for your generous intentions. You will be interested in learning that the last visitor to Shakspeare's home before my arrival here was a Philadelphian; also the last guest whom I entertained in London before I left to deliver my address in Birmingham (which was on the History of the United States) was your excellent Minister, Mr. John Welsh.

"We have been much gratified in England by the sympathy shown in America for our Queen.

"Yours, with all kind remembrances,

"A. P. STANLEY."

This was the last communication which MR. CHILDS received from the Very Reverend Dean of Westminster on the subject of the Shakspearian Memorial Window, it being understood between them that a window such as recommended should be placed in the Church of Holy Trinity, Dean Stanley undertaking to have it designed and executed.

The onerous and exacting character of his public duties prevented the Dean proceeding immediately with the work, and it was not long afterward that failing health interfered with his purpose, and his death, which occurred in mid-July of 1881, brought to a close for the time being the intention of MR. CHILDS to carry out his reverend and venerable friend's suggestion.

In 1886, however, it was proposed, and a Committee was appointed by some of the most distinguished lovers of Shakspeare in England, to restore the church at Stratford-upon-Avon in which the bones of Shakspeare lie. Appeals for contributions to secure the execution of this object were made, not only to the cultivated people of Great Britain, but to those of the United States as well. Among others who were greatly interested in the plan of restoration was James Macaulay, M.D., an honored and esteemed British scholar. Dr. Macaulay, who is one of the oldest friends of MR. CHILDS, personally appealed to him to contribute to the Restoration Fund. To this appeal MR. CHILDS promptly replied that he would give whatever sum Dr. Macaulay should suggest as desirable and befitting; but before an answer was received to this generous offer the Restoration Committee disagreed in respect of the character and extent of the work to be done, and the entire scheme failed of accomplishment. Subsequently, on September 9, 1886, Dr. Macaulay wrote to MR. CHILDS, acquainting him with the failure of the Committee to carry out the contemplated alteration or restoration of Holy Trinity Church, and advising him that the request for a contribution to that object was withdrawn. In this letter Dr. Macaulay, however, suggested that, if his friend had yet a desire as an American to pay tribute to the genius of Shakspeare in his own town, he could do it in no better way than by erecting a drinking fountain to his memory, " to be placed in the Market Square, where there is none, and which would be a handsome thing from an American." Dr. Macaulay added : " I think I once suggested this to you, and that it might be associated with Shakspeare by a motto taken from his works. It would be a useful gift both to man and beast."

Mr. Childs, it appears, accepted this suggestion readily, it being in happy accord with the spirit in which he had previously contributed the Memorial Window to the genius of the Christian poets, Herbert and Cowper, in Westminster Abbey, and subsequently, the Milton Window, in St. Margaret's, Westminster. It evidently seemed to him to afford another opportunity to add to the ties of fraternity and friendship between England and America, an object which appeared most desirable, and which being accomplished in the Queen's Jubilee Year would have the greater significance as being a recognition by Americans of **Victoria's brilliant and useful** reign of **half a century.**

THE MEETING OF THE COUNCIL.

Mr. Childs's hearty compliance with Dr. Macaulay's suggestion was communicated by the latter gentleman to Sir Arthur Hodgson, the Mayor of Stratford-upon-Avon, who, on the 15th of December, wrote to him as follows:—

"My Dear Sir: Many thanks for your kind letter: the name of Mr. Childs is no great surprise to me, and I shall be delighted to announce his most generous offer, which will supply a much and long needed want in this Borough, and to move the acceptance of Mr. Childs's offer at the meeting of my Council on the 21st instant."

On the next day notification was sent by the Town Clerk to the members of the Corporation Council: "The Mayor requests your attendance at a special meeting of the Council to be holden at the Town Hall, on Tuesday, the 21st day of December instant, at 11.30 o' the clock in the forenoon precisely, where the following business is proposed to be enacted: . . . .

"The Mayor to read a letter dated December 8th, 1886, from James Macaulay, Esq., M.D., the editor of 'The Leisure Hour,' London, conveying an offer from GEORGE W. CHILDS, Esq., of Philadelphia, to the Mayor and Corporation of Stratford-upon-Avon of a Public Drinking Fountain as 'the gift of an American citizen to the town of Shakspeare in the Jubilee Year of Queen Victoria.'

"The Mayor to move that MR. CHILDS's kind and generous offer be accepted, with grateful thanks, by this Corporation."

On the 22d of December Sir Arthur Hodgson wrote to Dr. Macaulay the following letter:—

"My Dear Sir: I have much pleasure in enclosing copy of a resolution unanimously and with acclamation adopted yesterday at a full and special meeting of the Council of the Corporation of Stratford-upon-Avon."

The resolution above referred to is herewith subjoined:—

"That MR. GEORGE W. CHILDS's (of Philadelphia) kind and generous offer of a Public Drinking Fountain, 'a gift to the Corporation of Stratford-upon-Avon of an American citizen in the Jubilee Year of Queen Victoria,' be accepted by the Corporation with grateful thanks."

The London 'Times,' of the 22d of December, under the caption of "The Queen's Jubilee," gave the subjoined account of the Council's proceedings:—

"At a meeting of the Stratford-upon-Avon Town Council, yesterday afternoon, a letter was read from Dr. Macaulay, editor of 'The Leisure Hour,' stating that he was authorized by MR. GEORGE W. CHILDS, of Philadelphia, to offer for the acceptance of the Corporation a handsome drinking fountain as the gift of an American citizen to the town of Shakspeare in the Jubilee Year of Queen Victoria. MR. CHILDS expressed the hope that the fountain would be evidence of the good-will of the two nations who have the fame and works of the poet as their common heritage. Dr. Macaulay added that Mr. Samuel Timmins, of Birmingham, had kindly undertaken to obtain from an eminent architect designs of the proposed structure for the approval of the Town Council. The Corporation passed a hearty resolution of thanks to MR. CHILDS for his munificent gift."

On the day after the passage of this resolution the 'New York Herald' published from its London correspondent the following special cable dispatch:—

"The Corporation of Stratford-upon-Avon has

voted the heartiest thanks of the town to MR. GEORGE W. CHILDS, of Philadelphia, for his gift of a Drinking Fountain to the place. In his letter presenting the gift MR. CHILDS expresses the hope that the fountain will prove an evidence of good-will between the two nations having the fame and works of Shakspeare as a common heritage."

With reference to this despatch, on its editorial page, the 'Herald,' in its issue of the same date, said :—

"MR. GEORGE W. CHILDS has given a drinking fountain to Stratford-upon-Avon, 'as evidence of good-will between the two nations having the fame and works of Shakspeare as a common heritage.'

"It was a graceful act on the part of MR. CHILDS, and is gracefully acknowledged by the Corporation of Stratford-upon-Avon, as will be seen in our foreign despatches. Such little acts of courtesy are not the least effective of incidents in sustaining pleasant international relations."

On December 24, 1886, the same journal published the subjoined special despatch from its Stratford correspondent :—

"STRATFORD-UPON-AVON, December 23, 1886. The name of the great American philanthropist,

GEORGE W. CHILDS, will henceforth be associated here with the name of Shakspeare.

"At the meeting of the Town Council on Tuesday the Mayor, Sir Arthur Hodgson, while stating that MR. CHILDS had offered to present Shakspeare's birthplace with a magnificent drinking fountain in honor of the Queen's Jubilee, referring to a letter which he held in his hand, added: 'The donor simply asks the Corporation to furnish water, and at night lights. MR. CHILDS would submit to the Corporation several designs for their choice, and he suggested that the fountain should be dedicated, either on the next birthday of the poet, or on June 20, the anniversary of the Queen's accession to the throne fifty years before.'

"Alderman Bird, amid renewed cheers for America and MR. CHILDS, seconded the Mayor's motion of acceptance and thanks. In the course of some very eulogistic remarks concerning the donor the Alderman said: 'The latter's generosities are widely known to the civilized world. Especially, Englishmen remembered MR. CHILDS's gift of an American Window to Westminster Abbey in memory of the poets Herbert and Cowper, which had an additional interest from the fact that the late Dean Stanley furnished the inscription to it.'"

After a conference the Council agreed to devote Jubilee Day to the ceremonies of receiving the gift.

The 'Illustrated London News' of February 26th contained the ensuing reference to the gift by the eminent author, George Augustus Sala:—

"Mr. G. W. Childs, of Philadelphia, U. S. A., well known, not only for his enterprise as a newspaper proprietor, but for the splendid hospitality which he has so long dispensed to travellers in the States—he was the friend of Dickens and of Thackeray—has made a graceful and generous Jubilee gift to the town of Stratford-upon-Avon. Some time since, Mr. Childs offered through Dr. Macaulay, the editor of 'The Leisure Hour,' to present a drinking fountain to Stratford, as the offering of an American citizen to the town of Shakspeare in the Jubilee Year of the good Queen Victoria. The offer was gratefully accepted by the Corporation; and a few days since the site for the fountain was fixed upon by a committee of taste, including the Mayor, Dr. Macaulay, Mr. Sam Timmins, Mr. Charles Flower, and several members of the Town Council, accompanied by the Borough Surveyor. It was finally decided to erect the fountain in the large open space in Rother

Street, which is midway between the Great Western Railway Station and the central part of the town.

"Mr. G. W. Childs has already won golden opinions of the English people by his munificence in placing in Westminster Abbey a noble window of stained glass in memory of two English poets and worthies, George Herbert and William Cowper.

"G. A. SALA."

THE SITE AND DESIGN SELECTED.

On February 17, 1887, the 'New York Herald's' special correspondent at Stratford-upon-Avon cabled the subjoined particulars with regard to the proposed gift:—

"Sir Arthur Hodgson, the Mayor, Dr. Macaulay, editor of 'The Leisure Hour,' the friend and correspondent of Mr. George W. Childs, with members of the local Town Council, met here to-day and decided upon the site and the design for a drinking fountain, which is the Jubilee gift of Mr. Childs to Shakspeare's town. As hitherto cabled to the 'Herald,' the design is by the architect Cossins, of Birmingham. The structure will be of granite, sixty feet high, the base being twenty-eight feet in diameter, and in the upper part four. It is to be faced by an antique clock, with an archway under the centre cut through the base and wide enough for one vehicle. Underneath, beside a drinking trough for horses, is a smaller one for dogs. At the entrances are cups.

"Upon the panel of the base is the inscription, 'The gift of an American citizen, GEORGE WILLIAM CHILDS, of Philadelphia, to the town of Shakspeare, in the Jubilee Year of Queen Victoria.' There are to be four mottoes cast. One will be from Washington Irving's description of Stratford-upon-Avon; another will be this Shakspearian line from Timon, 'Honest water that ne'er left any man in the mire.' The remaining two are not yet known. They are probably to be selected by MR. CHILDS.

"The design harmonizes well with the principal tower of the Shakspearian memorial buildings. The site is in the open market-place, near Rother Street, midway between the centre of the town and the great railway station, and within five minutes' walk of Shakspeare's house and the churchyard."

The Council of Stratford proceeded with the work with commendable energy. In its mid-month issue of the following June the 'Illustrated London News' published a sketch of the fountain, accompanied by the subjoined interesting description of it, which the 'New York World' published a fortnight later:—

"A lofty, spire-like, and highly ornamental drinking-fountain, with clock tower, is now being built in the Rother Market, Stratford-upon-Avon, at the cost of MR. GEORGE W. CHILDS, of Philadelphia, an American citizen, who, by this munificent and noble gift to the birthplace of Shakspeare, supplies the inhabitants of the town with what has long been felt to be one of its most pressing needs. It will be a durable and beautiful memorial of the friendly feeling existing between the two nations in this Jubilee Year of our Queen. The base of the tower is square on plan, with the addition of boldly projecting buttresses placed diagonally at the four corners, terminating with acutely pointed gablets surmounted by a lion bearing the arms of Great Britain alternately with the American eagle associated with the Stars and Stripes. On the north face is a polished granite basin, having the outline of a large segment of a circle, into which a stream of water is to flow constantly from a bronze spout; on the east and west sides are large troughs, of the same general outline and material, for the use of horses and cattle, and beneath these smaller troughs for sheep and dogs. On the south side is a door affording admission to the interior, flanked by two shallow niches, in one of which will be placed a barometer and in the other a thermometer, both of the best construction. Immediately over the basins and the door are moulded pointed arches, springing from dwarf columns, with carved capitals. The tympanum of each arch is filled by geometric tracery, profusely enriched with carvings of foliage.

"The next story of the tower has on each face a triple arcade with moulded pointed trefoiled arches on slender shafts. The arches are glazed, and light a small chamber, in which the clock is to be placed. At the corners are cylindrical turrets, terminating in conical spirelets in two stages, the surfaces of the cones enriched with scale-like ornament. In the next story are the four dials of the clock, under crocketed gables, with finials representing 'Puck,' 'Mustard-seed,' 'Peas-blossom,' and 'Cobweb.' The clock-faces project slightly from a cylindrical tower flanked by four other smaller three-quarter attached turrets of the same plan; from the main central cylinder springs a spire of a slightly concave outline, and the four turrets have similar but much smaller spirelets, all five springing from the same level, and all terminating in lofty gilded vanes. Immediately below the line of springing is a band of panelling formed of narrow trefoiled arches. The central spire has on four opposite sides gableted spire-lights, and, at about one-third of its height, a continuous band of narrow lights to spread the sound of the clock bells. The height from the road to the top of the vane is sixty feet. The clock will be illuminated at night.

"The materials of which the monument is being constructed are of the most durable kind—Peterhead granite for the base and troughs, and for the superstructure a very hard and durable stone of a delicate gray color from Bolton Wood, in Yorkshire."

THE DEDICATORY POEM.

Mr. Childs, naturally desiring that the name of an American poet should be associated with the dedication of the memorial, suggested to Dr. Oliver Wendell Holmes, whose sympathies for the great master of the English Drama are known to lie so broad and deep, that he should write a poem appropriate to the occasion. The good and genial poet at first stoutly demurred, pleading that his muse, like himself, was growing old and delighted most in restful, inactive ease by the sea. But, being further urged, Dr. Holmes, on the 17th day of August, 1887, wrote from Beverly Farms, Massachusetts, to his old friend in these words:—

"DEAR MR. CHILDS:

"I have written a poem for the celebration of the opening of the fountain.

"There are nine verses, each of nine lines, as it now stands. I mean to revise it carefully, transcribe it, and send you the copy in the course of this week.

"I have taken pains with it and I hope you will like it. Please do not take the trouble of replying before you get the poem.

"Always truly yours,

"O. W. HOLMES."

Two days later the poem as it appears in the subsequent accounts of the celebration was received by MR. CHILDS. Its many classical allusions testify as much to the generous culture of the author's mind as does the rare beauty of his verse to his poetic genius.

A TRIBUTE TO "CHILDS AT AVON."

In the Brooklyn 'Eagle' there appeared while the Fountain was still building, under the caption of

"CHILDS AT AVON," an article as brilliant in manner as it was scholarly in matter. The writer, who modestly hid his identity under the initial H., and of whose paper we make this free, brief abstract, said: "If no Shakspeare had been born and lived and died at Stratford-upon-Avon, I should still remember it as one of the most charming spots in Warwickshire. Often when staying at Leamington have I set out early on a summer morning and spent my day by the banks of Avon and visited the house where he was born, including the low ceiling bedroom in which he first saw the light when Mary Arden brought him into the world in which, after his death, he was to be the most mysterious and inspired of teachers. Many an hour have I spent in the beautiful parish church of Holy Trinity at Stratford, reading the epitaph upon his grave and feeling with a much-sneered-at poet, 'Satan' Montgomery, whom Macaulay so pitilessly criticised, that I, for once, could

"'Tread the ground by genius often trod,
Nor feel a nature more akin to God.'

"The gift of MR. GEORGE W. CHILDS, of Philadelphia, of a public drinking fountain in honor of Shakspeare, to the town of Stratford-upon-Avon, is memorable as being a tribute to the Queen of Shakspeare's nation on her jubilee.

"The first thought that strikes me—for I leave the noble benefactions of Mr. Childs for the latter part of this article—is how the immortal Shakspeare would have stood amazed had he beheld this grand water fountain erected to his memory Although he praises water in the words 'Honest water that ne'er left any man in the mire,' which is to be one of the inscriptions on Mr. Childs's memorial drinking fountain, the habits of his time were certainly not in favor of water as a beverage. There were many in that age, like Sir Walter Raleigh, who abhorred drunkenness and denounced it with as much emphasis as King James I. did the tobacco which Raleigh extolled with enthusiasm. But it would have taken a long journey, I think, to have found a teetotaler in England in the days of Shakspeare. 'Good Queen Bess' drank ale at breakfast. King James rolled drunk from his throne. Shakspeare himself was thoroughly convivial, though not a drinker to excess. He lived like the men of his time, enjoyed his social glass of sack or canary with Ben Jonson, or Burbage and other authors or actors, and, no doubt, sometimes woke with a headache next morning. There is nothing disrespectful to his memory to say that his early death at the age of 52 has been generally attributed to the effects of a convivial evening. A recent Shakspearian enthusiast, Mrs. Dall, says, in her 'Handbook to Shakspeare:' 'The pleasant days went on for a few weeks. Jonson and Drayton came to see Shakspeare, and very likely went to the old inn where he had been accustomed to watch the antics of a "fool," that he might immortalize him in the company of Sly, Naps, Turf, and Pimpernell. The hilarity of the party had attracted the attention of the villagers, for when, in March, 1616, the poet was stricken with fever, the rumor ran that it came from too much drinking with his friends.' 'He died on the 23d of April.

"But if, as I have ventured to suggest, Shakspeare would have been amazed at a water fountain erected to his memory, he would probably have been still more astonished at such poor relations as dogs and horses participating with his fellow-citizens in the benefit of it. Such is Mr. Childs's arrangement, and I think it indicates the true humanity of his nature. The dog is the only animal that will forsake his own kind for the sake of man and will die upon his master's grave. There are miscreants and scoundrels in all races, and the canine is not an exception. But there are as many virtuous dogs as virtuous men, and from them we may learn affection, patience, long-suffering, unselfishness, and friendship and fidelity till death. No wonder that the poor Indian of Pope's 'Essay on Man,'

> "'Whose soul proud Science never taught to stray
> Far as the solar walk or milky way,
>
> *   *   *   *   *   *
>
> Yet thinks, admitted to that equal sky,
> His faithful dog shall bear him company.'

"Let us hope that if the great soul of Shakspeare looks down at Queen Victoria's Jubilee on Stratford-upon-Avon he will approve of Mr. Childs's munificent gift to the corporation of which his family, especially his father, John Shakspeare, were ancient and honorable members, even though it has embraced the thirsty souls of dogs and horses as well as of men, women, and children.

"Of Mr. Childs, whom I have never seen, it is impossible for any public-spirited mind of any nationality to think too highly. He is not a flatterer of English noblemen, but a benefactor, first to his own people and then a hospitable host to distinguished foreigners. In fact, Mr. Childs is way ahead in wealth and respectability of most of the notables to whom he has extended his hospitality. Beginning as an errand boy, when he went from Baltimore to Philadelphia, in mere childhood, he became printer, bookseller, publisher, and newspaper proprietor, by that resolute virtue of perseverance and honesty which overcomes the world, and while some may envy his prosperity, no one can dispute that he has earned it by a life of integrity and industry such as few even in America have equalled. Upon the fountain in honor of Shakspeare at Stratford-upon-Avon will stand the words, 'The gift of an American citizen;' and this reminds me of the words of the late Dean Stanley, when he visited this country for the first and only time in 1878, referring to Mr. Childs's Memorial Window in his abbey to George Herbert and William Cowper: 'There is in Westminster Abbey a window dear to American hearts because erected by an honored citizen of Philadelphia.' It might seem strange that the gift should be made in the Centennial Year of American Independence, but Mr. Childs has the right idea of the commonwealth of letters, and believes that the great writers of the English tongue belong to the Anglo-Saxon and English-speaking races, wherever they may be; and as he did honor to George Herbert and William Cowper, so now he has done honor to the greater name of Shakspeare, who belongs to no country, but is the admiration of all civilized races.

"Mr. George W. Childs's fountain completes the homage which Americans have paid to Shakspeare. Years ago, when I talked to an old woman who showed me over the house he was born in, she said, in answer to a question, that Americans seemed to take most interest in it. The case of Miss Delia Bacon is most pathetic, although I believe it was not her Baconian theory which made her so unhappy. She was a woman of singular talent, coming from one of the most big-brained families of New England. An early disappointment had made her feel the need of an eccentric enthusiasm, and by the kind and very unusual permission of the Vicar of Stratford she was allowed to pass whole nights in the church wherein the bones were laid, which he forbade strangers to remove, but not to keep their vigils by. Although Miss Bacon was hallucinated, her 'Philosophy of Shakspeare's Plays,' introduced by Hawthorne, elicited the praise of Ralph Waldo Emerson. Her special vagary was that Shakspeare had not been Shakspeare and that Francis Bacon was the real Shakspeare, and so the idol of her mind was destroyed by her own imagination. As

I said, she was not alone in this ridiculous theory, but it is sad to think of the lonely, enthusiastic woman worshiping night and day at the shrine of a god whom she would end by disbelieving in altogether. Yet Samuel Taylor Coleridge was not much wiser when he said of Shakspeare, 'Does God inspire an idiot?'

"Mr. Childs's gift and its acceptance by the corporation of Stratford set the seal, at any rate, to our American belief in the identity as well as the greatness of Shakspeare. His will more than ever be the shrine which American travellers, with Washington Irving's description of Stratford in their hands, will visit. It is said that in Virginia, in a churchyard sheltered by southern foliage, there is a tombstone with the inscription commemorative of a man who died in the seventeenth century: 'One of the pall-bearers of William Shakspeare.' The only relic of the man I have read of is a pair of gauntlets possessed by an American, one of the most eminent and honored of Shakspearian scholars and critics, Dr. Horace Howard Furness, of Philadelphia. If it be so, it only confirms the fact that the Americans have been his greatest and most dispassionate admirers, even if the Germans were the first to discern his singular yet universal genius, and are still the most enthusiastic witnesses of his plays. In France, also, M. Taine and other great writers, including Victor Hugo, **have been** earnest lovers of Shakspeare; but when English or American tragic actors have played his principal characters in Paris they have found far less appreciative audiences than they have in Berlin or Frankfort or any other German city. At any rate, MR. CHILDS has helped to make one picturesque little town by a beautiful river in England more famous than even Shakspeare's name had made it before, and henceforward no one who visits England will leave it without spending a few hours, at least, in the quiet town of Stratford-upon-Avon."

THE FOUNTAIN DEDICATED.

On October 17, 1887, **the fountain** was dedicated with imposing ceremony, an exhaustive report of which was published on the following Friday, in the Stratford-upon-Avon 'Herald,' and which **is here** presented anew from that journal:—

"All things combined to give *éclat* to the important event of Monday last—the inauguration of the handsome fountain given by MR. CHILDS, of Philadelphia. It was a happy thought of that prominent and respected citizen to arrange that this splendid memorial of American admiration for and sympathy with England's greatest poet should take place in the Jubilee Year of Queen Victoria's reign; and it was also a happy idea to secure the greatest of English actors to carry out the important function. So distinguished an assemblage of gentlemen has rarely come together in Stratford-upon-Avon. Art, literature, and the drama were well represented, and the ceremonial was one of international interest. The fountain forms both a welcome and substantial benefit to the town, and a graceful addition to its many points of natural and historic interest. Stratford accepted the bequest with a heartiness at once agreeable to the giver, and illustrative of the friendly feeling of Warwickshire for the people of the great Republic of the West.

"Preparations for the celebration of the event were made on Saturday. The scaffolding, which so long impeded a full view of the fountain, was removed, the final touches were put to the stonework of the elegant erection, and a tent was erected in which the ceremony was to take place in the event of the weather proving unpropitious. Mr. Irving, who performed the inaugural ceremony, arrived in Stratford the previous day, and was the guest of Mr. Charles E. Flower, at Avonbank. The distinguished actor only finished his Liverpool engagement on Saturday night, this being the last place on his provincial tour before his departure for America. On Sunday morning he travelled to Blisworth, *via* Rugby, a special train on the East and West Junction Railway meeting him at the former place. On his arrival at Stratford he received a very cordial welcome. A large number of people had assembled on the platform and outside the building, and, as soon as he emerged from the railway carriage and was recognized, a very vigorous cheer was given. He was met by Mr. **Flower**, and proceeded at once to Avonbank.

" Monday morning, as we have said, opened most auspiciously. The sun soon dispersed the early mist, and at noon, the time fixed for the ceremony, there was almost an unclouded sky, and in the splendid autumn light the fountain showed itself to perfection. The rich light gray stone seemed to reflect the sun's rays, and the vane, which caps the edifice, shone with great brilliancy. The fountain was complete, with one exception—the clock faces were there, but not the hands. Sir Arthur Hodgson (the Mayor), in accepting MR. CHILDS's munificent gift, arranged for an inaugural ceremonial befitting its international as well as its practical character. Sir Arthur issued invitations on a scale of imposing hospitality, and the Clopton House was filled with a number of distinguished guests. Shortly before twelve o'clock a procession was arranged at the Town Hall, the local volunteers with their drum-and-fife band forming the lead, and followed by the Snitterfield brass band. Then came the Mayor, on each side of whom walked the Lord High Steward (Earl de La Warr) and his Excellency the American Minister (Mr. Phelps). **Mr.** Henry Irving, accom**panied** by his secretary, **Mr.** Bram **Stoker, came next,** and **then succeeded** the Mayors of Leamington, **Warwick, Coventry,** and Lichfield, wearing their gold chains of office. The members of the Corporation and their officers brought up the rear, those present being Aldermen Bird, **Cox,** Newton, R. Gibbs, E. Gibbs, and Colbourne; Councillors Flower, Cole, Eaves, Rogers, Birch, C. Green, Hawkes, L. Greene, Maries, Kemp, and Morris. The streets during the moving of the procession presented a very animated appearance, there being a liberal display of bunting throughout the route. Arriving at the site of the Memorial, **they** found assembled a very large concourse of persons, all anxious to witness the proceedings, and to listen to the eloquence of the great

English actor. His address was delivered in the silvery tones **so** familiar to those who have seen and heard Mr. Irving on the stage. He was studiously brief, but what a large amount of feeling **and** meaning his few words contained! The inaugural speech over, the water was turned on, and the fountain **was** dedicated to the public for **ever**. Cheers followed the announcement, and the formal ceremony soon came to an end. Everything had been happily done, and the fraternal relations of the two **great** nations which regard the works of Shakspeare as a common heritage were **thus** increasingly cemented. There were mutual congratulations; common **praise** of MR. CHILDS's magnificent gift, of the architect's skill and taste, of the builder's sound workmanship. The whole proceedings were happily conceived **and** successfully carried out.

THE LOWELL AND **WHITTIER LETTERS.**

"The speeches at the fountain and at the luncheon which followed are fully recorded below.

"The Mayor announced that he had received letters explaining inability to attend from the High Sheriff, the Lord Lieutenant, Lord and Lady Hertford, his Excellency the American Minister **at** Paris, the Secretary of Legation of the United States, Sir Stafford Northcote, the Dean of Queen's College, Oxford, and Mr. Halliwell-Phillipps. His Worship afterwards read the following letters from Mr. James Russell Lowell and Mr. J. G. Whittier :—

"' DEAR SIR ARTHUR HODGSON:

"'I should more deeply regret my inability to be present at the interesting ceremonial of the 17th were it not that my countrymen will be more fitly and adequately represented there by our accomplished Minister, Mr. Phelps.

"'The occasion is certainly most interesting. The monument which you accept to-day in behalf of your townsmen commemorates at once the most marvellous of Englishmen and the Jubilee Year of the august lady whose name is honored wherever the language is spoken of which he was the greatest master. No symbol could more aptly serve this double purpose than a fountain; for surely no poet ever " poured forth so broad a river of speech" as he —whether he was the author of the Novum Organum also or not—nor could the purity of her character and example be better typified than by the current that shall flow forever from the sources opened here to-day.

"'It was Washington Irving who first embodied in his delightful English the emotion which Stratford-upon-Avon awakens in the heart of the pilgrim, and especially of the American pilgrim, who visits it. I am glad to think that this Memorial should be the gift of an American, and thus serve to recall the kindred blood of two great nations, joint heirs of the same noble language and of the genius that has given it a cosmopolitan significance. I am glad of it because it is one of the multiplying signs that these two nations are beginning to think more and more of the things in which they sympathize, less and less of those in which they differ.

"'A common language is not, indeed, the surest bond of amity, for this enables each country to understand whatever unpleasant thing the other may chance to say about it. As I am one of those who believe that an honest friendship between England and America is a most desirable thing, I trust that we shall on both sides think it equally desirable, in our intercourse one with another, to make our mother-tongue search her coffers round for the polished rather than the sharp-cornered epithets she has stored there. Let us by all means speak the truth to each other, for there is no one else who can speak it to either of us with such a fraternal instinct for the weak point of the other; but let us do it in such wise as to show that it is the truth we love, and not the discomfort we can inflict by means of it. Let us say agreeable things to each other and of each other whenever we conscientiously can. My friend, Mr. Childs, has said one of these agreeable things in a very solid and durable way. A common literature and a common respect for certain qualities of character and ways of thinking supply a neutral ground where we may meet in the assurance that we shall find something amiable in each other, and from being less than kind become more than kin.

"'In old maps the line which outlined the British Possessions in America included the greater part of what is now the territory of the United States. The possessions of the American in England are laid down on no map, yet he holds them of memory and imagination by a title such as no conquest ever established and no revolution can ever overthrow. The dust that is sacred to you is sacred to him. The annals which Shakspeare makes walk before us in flesh and blood are his no less than yours. These are the ties which we recognize, and are glad to recognize on occasions like this. They will be yearly drawn closer as Science goes on with her work of abolishing Time and Space, and thus renders more easy that "peaceful commerce 'twixt dividable shores" which is so potent to clear away whatever is exclusive in nationality or savors of barbarism in patriotism.

"'I remain, dear Mr. Mayor, faithfully yours,

"'J. R. LOWELL.'

"'OAK KNOLL, DANVERS, MASS., 6th Mo., 30th, 1887.
"'MR. G. W. CHILDS.

"'DEAR FRIEND: I have just read of thy noble and appropriate gift to the birthplace of Shakspeare. It was a happy thought to connect it with the Queen's Jubilee. It will make for peace between the two great kindred nations, and will go far to atone for the foolish abuse of England by too many of our party orators and papers. As an American, and proud of the name, I thank thee for expressing in this munificent way the true feeling of our people.

"'I am very truly, thy friend,

"'JOHN G. WHITTIER.'

A BRIEF HISTORY.

"The letters having been read, the Mayor then said he must say a few words about the history of the fountain. It came about in this way. It had originally been suggested to Mr. Childs of Philadelphia, by an eminent English divine and scholar (the late Dean Stanley), that it would be a good and graceful thing for an American to do to leave his mark in the historic borough wherein Shakspeare was born, and lived, and died, and was buried. After the death of the Dean nothing more was said of the project until Mr. Childs's friend, Dr. Macaulay, wrote to him expressing the same idea which had been four years before presented to the giver of the Herbert and Cowper Window to Westminster Abbey; but Dr. Macaulay urged that the best gift would be a drinking fountain, of which Stratfordians stood very much in want. All of Mr. Childs's numerous letters respecting the fountain, extending over twelve months, evinced a spirit of affection for dear old England, and a feeling of deep regard for our most gracious Queen. Therefore we chose the Jubilee Year for the presentation. In all this Mr. Childs has proved that blood is stronger than water. Yes, in this case blood is stronger than water. Mr. Childs had imbued his feelings, English and American—mixed them up together, as it were. Then, of course, they had to make their arrangements. He did not hesitate to say that, if it had not been for Dr. Macaulay, and the valuable assistance he gave, they could not have proved the fountain, as he believed they intended to do that day, a success. Dr. Macaulay helped them heartily, and he felt deeply grateful for his valuable assistance. Then came the question—who should inaugurate the stately Memorial, and Dr. Macaulay and himself both agreed that they could not choose a better man than their celebrated English tragedian, **Mr. Henry Irving**. They were not at all sure of securing the valuable presence of his Excellency, Mr. Phelps, the American Minister in this country, and thought it better to be sure of their ground. However, he was there, and Mr. Irving, and on behalf of the borough of Stratford-upon-Avon and the Corporation, of which he had the honor to be Mayor, he returned to them their most grateful thanks for having come amongst them on that auspicious occasion. He knew very well that Mr. Phelps had travelled night and day from the north of Scotland to be present, not only to lend his countenance to the gathering, but to indorse the munificent act of his noble countryman. It was, again, a great satisfaction to the people of Stratford to be able to secure the services of the great tragedian, who, they were glad to know, was one of the trustees of Shakspeare's Birthplace. They thanked Mr. Irving for coming among them, and would conclude his remarks by asking Mr. Irving to dedicate the noble fountain to the borough of Stratford-upon-Avon for ever.

POET TO POET.

"Mr. Irving, on stepping forward, was received with great cheering. He said he had been requested to read a poem which had been dedicated to the fountain at Stratford-upon-Avon—a poem written by a man who was loved wherever the English language was spoken."

Mr. Irving then read the following poem by Oliver Wendell Holmes :—

> Welcome, thrice welcome, is thy silvery gleam,
>   Thou long-imprisoned stream!
> Welcome the tinkle of thy crystal beads
> As plashing raindrops to the flowery meads,
> As summer's breath to Avon's whispering reeds!
> From rock-walled channels, drowned in rayless night,
>   Leap forth to life and light;
> Wake from the darkness of thy troubled dream,
> And greet with answering smile the morning's beam!
>
> No purer lymph the white-limbed Naiad knows
>   Than from thy chalice flows;
> Not the bright spring of Afric's sunny shores,
> Starry with spangles washed from golden ores,
> Nor glassy stream Blandusia's fountain pours,

Nor wave translucent where Sabrina fair
    Braids her loose-flowing hair,
Nor the swift current, stainless as it rose
Where chill Arveiron steals from Alpine snows.

Here shall the traveller stay his weary feet
    To seek thy calm retreat;
Here at high noon the brown-armed reaper rest;
Here, when the shadows, lengthening from the west,
Call the mute song-bird to his leafy nest,
Matron and maid shall chat the cares away
    That brooded o'er the day,
While flocking round them troops of children meet,
And all the arches ring with laughter sweet.

Here shall the steed, his patient life who spends
    In toil that never ends,
Hot from his thirsty tramp o'er hill and plain,
Plunge his red nostrils, while the torturing rein
Drops in loose loops beside his floating mane;
Nor the poor brute that shares his master's lot
    Find his small needs forgot,—
Truest of humble, long-enduring friends,
Whose presence cheers, whose guardian care defends!

Here lark and thrush and nightingale shall sip,
    And skimming swallows dip,
And strange shy wanderers fold their lustrous plumes
Fragrant from bowers that lent their sweet perfumes
Where Pæstum's rose or Persia's lilac blooms;
Here from his cloud the eagle stoop to drink
    At the full basin's brink,

And whet his beak against its rounded lip,
His glossy feathers glistening **as they drip.**

Here shall the dreaming poet linger long,
    Far from his listening throng,—
Nor lute nor lyre his trembling hand shall bring;
Here no frail Muse shall imp her crippled wing,
No faltering minstrel strain his throat to sing!
These hallowed echoes who shall dare to claim
    Whose tuneless voice would shame,
Whose jangling chords with jarring notes would wrong
The nymphs that heard the Swan of Avon's song?

What **visions** greet the pilgrim's **raptured eyes!**
    What ghosts made real rise!
The dead return,—they breathe,—they live again,
Joined by **the host of Fancy's** airy train,
Fresh from the springs of Shakspeare's quickening **brain!**
The stream that slakes the soul's diviner thirst
    Here found the sunbeams first;
Rich with his fame, not less shall memory **prize**
The gracious gift that humbler wants supplies.

O'er the wide waters reached the hand that **gave**
    To all this bounteous wave,
With health and strength and joyous beauty fraught;
Blest be the generous pledge of friendship, brought
From the far home of brothers' love, unbought!
Long may fair Avon's fountain flow, enrolled
    With storied shrines of old,
Castalia's spring, Egeria's **dewy cave,**
And Horeb's rock the God of Israel clave!

Land of our Fathers, ocean makes us two,
  But heart to heart is true!
Proud is your towering daughter in the West,
Yet in her burning life-blood reign confest
Her mother's pulses beating in her breast.
This holy fount, whose rills from heaven descend,
  Its gracious drops shall lend—
Both foreheads bathed in that baptismal dew,
And love make one the old home and the new!

THE MEMORIAL ORATOR.

" Mr. Irving then spoke as follows : ' The occasion which has drawn us here to-day has an exceptional interest and a special significance. We have met to celebrate a tribute which has been paid to the memory of Shakspeare by an American citizen, and which is associated with the Jubilee Year of our Queen. The donor of this beautiful monument I am happy to claim as a personal friend. MR. GEORGE W. CHILDS is not only an admirable specimen of the public spirit and enterprising energy of Philadelphia, but he is also a man who has endeared himself to a very wide circle by many generous deeds. I do not wonder at his munificence, for to men like him it is a second nature; but I rejoice in the happy inspiration which prompted a gift that so worthily represents the common homage of two great peoples to the most famous man of their common race. We are honored to-day by the presence of a distinguished American, the political representative of his country in England. But it would do far less than justice to Mr. Phelps to affirm that he is with us in any formal and diplomatic sense. On this spot, of all others, Americans cease to be aliens, for here they claim our kinship with the great master of English speech. It is not for me to say in Mr. Phelps's presence how responsive American life and literature are to the influence which has done more than the work of any other man to mould the thought and character of generations. The simplest records of Stratford show that this is the Mecca of American pilgrims, and that the place which gave birth to Shakspeare is regarded as the fountain of the mightiest and most enduring inspiration of our mother tongue. It is not difficult to believe that amongst the strangers who write those imposing letters U. S. A. in the visitors' book in the historic house hard by there are some whose colloquial speech still preserves many phrases which have come down from Shakspeare's time. Some idioms, which are supposed to be of American invention, can be traced back to Shakspeare. And we can imagine that in the audience at the old Globe Theatre there were ignorant and unlettered men who treasured up something of Shakspeare's imagery and vivid portraiture, and carried with them across the ocean thoughts and words, "solemn vision and bright silver dream," which helped to nurture their transplanted stock. For it is above all things as the poet of the people that Shakspeare is supreme. He wrote in days when literature made no appeal to the multitude. Books were for a limited class, but the theatre was open to all. How many Englishmen, to whom reading was a labor or an impossibility, must have drawn from the stage which Shakspeare had enriched some of the most priceless jewels of the human mind! One of the inscriptions on this fountain is, perhaps, the most expressive tribute to Shakspeare which the people's heart can pay: "Ten thousand honors and blessings on the bard who has gilded the dull realities of life with innocent illusions." Those simple words speak a gratitude far more eloquent and enduring than whole volumes of criticism. It is not only because Shakspeare is the delight of scholars, or because he has infinite charms for the refined, that he wields the unbroken staff of Prospero over the imagination of mankind. It is because his spell is woven from the truth and simplicity of Nature herself. There lies the heart of the mystery. Without an effort the simplest mind passes into the realms of Shakspeare's fancy. Learned and simple, gentle and humble, all may drink from the inexhaustible wisdom of this supreme sage. And so it seems to me that no happier emblem of Shakspeare's genius in his native place could have been chosen than this Memorial Fountain. I suppose we shall never be content with what little we know of Shakspeare's personal history. Yet we can see him in his home-life here, the man of genial manners and persuasive speech, unassuming and serene, and perhaps unconscious that he had created in the world of letters as great a marvel as his contemporary Galileo's discovery in the world of science. And we may conjure other fancies. We can picture Shakspeare returning from his bourne to find upon the throne a queen who rules with gentler sway than the great sovereign that he knew; and yet whose reign has glories more beneficent than those of Elizabeth. We can try to imagine his emotion when he finds "this dear England" he loved so well expanded beyond the seas; and we can at least be happy in the thought that when he had mastered the lessons of the conflict which divided us from our kinsmen in America, he would be proud to see in Stratford the gift of a distinguished American citizen—this memorial of our re-union under the shadow of his undying name.'

OUR CENTENNIAL GUEST.

"In response to a call from the Mayor, Sir Philip Cunliffe Owen, who was originally associated with the British Commission of the Centennial Exhibition of 1876, in Philadelphia, said that, as an old personal friend of Mr. Childs, he was gratified at being permitted to say a few words on that interesting occasion, and to express the gratitude of a large number of English people who had received Mr. Childs's hospitality. That hospitality was well known in that 'City of Brotherly Love'—Philadelphia—and Mr. Childs was beloved both over there and in this country. He was very pleased indeed that he should have been allowed in the name of those who loved Mr. Childs—as all who had met him in America did—to join with the orator who had just charmed them by his eloquence in expressing their gratitude for that noble gift.

TO THE MEMORY OF SHAKSPEARE.

"The water was then turned on, and, filling a cup, Mr. Irving drank 'To the Immortal Memory of Shakspeare,' while the Mayor announced to the company that the water had been pronounced by authority to be clear, palatable, and good. The band in the mean time played the National Anthem and 'Hail, Columbia,' while hearty cheers were afterwards given for the Queen, for the President of the United States, for the American Minister (Mr. Phelps), for Mr. CHILDS, the munificent donor of the fountain, for the Mayor and Lady Hodgson, and for Mr. Irving. This part of the proceedings then terminated.

THE MAYOR'S GUESTS.

"At one o'clock the Mayor entertained a large and distinguished company at luncheon in the upper room of the Town Hall. The guests of his Worship included the American Minister (Mr. Phelps), Earl De La Warr (High Steward of the Borough), Mr. Henry Irving, Mr. C. E. Flower, Mrs. C. E. Flower,

Lord Ronald **Gower,** Lady Hodgson, the Hon. **Mr. Hewitt,** Miss Hodgson, **Dr.** Macaulay, Mrs. Macaulay, Mr. Macaulay, **Jr.,** Sir Theodore Martin, K. C. B., **Sir** Philip Cunliffe **Owen, Mr. F.** Townsend, M. P., **Mrs.** Townsend, Rev. G. Arbuthnot, Mr. **Walter** (proprietor of the 'Times'), **Mrs.** Walter, **Councillor** Archer, Mr. T. Adkins, **Rev. F. H. Annesley, Mrs.** Annesley, Mrs. Arbuthnot, **Alderman Bird,** Councillor Birch, **the Borough Surveyor (Mr. A. T. Davies), the Borough Chamberlain (Mr. A. M.** Cox), Mr. R. Bridgman (the contractor), Mr. G. Boyden, Rev. W. Barnard, Mrs. Barnard, Mr. T. Brookes, Mr. E. S. Broadfield, Mr. W. Burns, Councillor Cole, **Councillor Canning, Mr. J. A. Cossins, Mrs. Cossins,** the Mayor of Coventry, **Miss** Carleton, **Miss Alice** Carleton, Mr. C. Caffin, **Mr. F. Crawford, Mr. J. H.** Caseley, the **Deputy-Mayor (Alderman Colbourne),** Councillor Eaves, Mr. **Edgar Flower, Mrs. Edgar Flower,** Mr. **A. D.** Flower, Miss Flower, **Col.** Feilden, Alderman **E.** Gibbs, Alderman **R.** Gibbs, Councillor C. Green, Councillor L. Greene, Mr. **C. R.** Garnet, Mr. F. Gibbs, Mr. D. S. Gregg, Mrs. Gregg, Councillor Hawkes, Councillor Hutchings, Mr. F. Hawley, Mr. J. Henson, Mr. W. Izod, Mr. J. C. Jones, Mrs. Cove Jones, Councillor Kemp, Mr. Kinnear, Rev. **R. S.** de C. Laffan, Mrs. Laffan, Lady Laffan, Mayor of

Leamington (Mr. S. T. Wackrill), Capt. Lupton, Mr. C. Lowndes, the Mayor of Lichfield, Mr. H. S. Loveday, Councillor H. Maries, Councillor T. Morris, Mr. Charles E. Martin, Mrs. Martin, Miss Minet, Mr. S. H. Mountford, Mr. F. A. Mountford, Alderman Newton, Mr. J. J. Nason, Mrs. Nason, Mr. T. W. Norbury, the Priest Chaplain (the Rev. F. Smith), Mrs. Porter, Mr. E. Pritchard, C. E., Mrs. Pomeroy, Mr. Pemberton, Councillor Rogers, Mr. Richardson, Mr. S. Sanders, Mrs. Sanders, Mrs. F. Smith, Mr. R. Savage, Mr. Bram Stoker, Mr. Clement Scott, the Town Clerk (Mr. T. Hunt), Mr. S. Timmins, Mr. Yates Thompson, Mrs. Yates Thompson, Councillor Whiteman, the Mayor of Warwick, Mr. J. E. Wilcox, Mr. J. C. Parkinson, Mr. F. Marshall, Mr. J. C. Warden, and Mr. H. White, of the American Legation, London.

THE TOASTS.

"The Mayor, in giving the toast of 'The Queen,' said it was one which, in this ancient, loyal, and historic borough, was always well received. This year Stratford had done its best to honor the Jubilee. By a happy coincidence, the foundation stone of the handsome fountain they had inaugurated that morning was laid on Jubilee Day by the Mayoress. They all felt that the Queen sat enthroned in the hearts of her subjects. He thought they might truly say that she was the most constitutional Sovereign who had ever reigned over them. Throughout her long and glorious reign we had had a government of the people by the people for the people. Of Victoria it might be said, as by Cranmer (in 'Henry VIII.') of another Queen, 'She shall be to the happiness of England an aged princess. Many days shall see her, yet not a day without a deed to crown it.'

"The toast was received with hearty cheers, after which the Mayor proposed 'The Prince and Princess of Wales and the rest of the Royal Family,' which met with an equally cordial reception.

"Earl De La Warr said he had great pleasure in proposing the next toast, 'The President of the United States.' They had that day witnessed a ceremony which had excited the liveliest interest of all who had the pleasure of being present. The function at which they had assisted that morning was more than a mere ceremony; it was an indication of the sympathy existing between England and America. He thought he was speaking the sentiments of the nation as well as of the borough when he said that they viewed that auspicious occasion, not only as a proof of the great interest which was felt in America in the memory of the immortal poet, but also as drawing more closely the bonds of unity and friendly feeling between the United States and this country.

"The toast was very cordially received.

THE ADDRESS OF THE AMERICAN MINISTER.

"His Excellency the American Minister, Mr. Phelps, who experienced a hearty greeting, said, in response :—

"'It is certainly a very grateful duty to respond to a sentiment honored by Americans everywhere and under all circumstances, which has been proposed in such felicitous terms by Lord De La Warr, and received so cordially by you all. And for the kind allusions to myself which I have heard to-day and for your more than kind reception, I can only offer you my thanks and my wish that they were better deserved. The manner in which the name of the President of the United States is always received when it is brought forward in an English company, and the kindness which everywhere is made to surround the path of his representative in this country, are exceedingly gratifying, because they are the expression, and the more significant because they are often the spontaneous expression, of the cordial, friendly feeling which animates the heart of the people of this country towards their kinsmen across that sea which used to divide but which now unites them. The relations between these two countries are not the property of themselves alone; they are the property of the civilized world. It would be a calamity **too** great to be anticipated, and which I trust may never be realized, to all the civilized world if these relations were to be severed. But it is to be **borne in mind** that they depend far less upon governments and public men than upon the spirit which animates the people on either side. Mr. Irving happily remarked this morning that I was not here in a diplomatic capacity. Diplomacy, that black art as it used to be known in the world, and I hope has ceased to be known, has very little place among the straightforward Saxon race. It cannot be too strongly borne in mind, I think, that it is on the cultivation of a friendly spirit on both sides that our cordial relations depend. So far as I have observed, people do not quarrel unless they desire it. When they are hostile, provocation is not far to seek; when they are friendly, there are very few provocations that will not somehow be patched up and adjusted. It is in the intercourse so admirably depicted in the letter of my predecessor, Mr. Lowell, by which the people of the two countries come to know each other and understand and appreciate each other, to partake of each other's hospitality, to enjoy with each other the amenities of social, personal, individual life, that the spirit arises that will always make these people friends. And it may be usefully remembered by those philanthropists and humanitarians who are anxious to preserve the peace of the world, that it is much better maintained by justice and kindness in the treatment of each other internationally than it is by obtaining paper promises that injustice and unkindness shall not be resented. Such promises are either worthless or needless. They are needless while nations are friendly; they are worthless while nations are hostile. It is one of the amenities to which I have alluded that brings us together here to-day. I must say a word, before I sit down, about the gift of my warm-hearted and distinguished countryman which has been inaugurated this morning. I should rather mar what you have already heard if I were to attempt to add much to what has been said, and so well said, by the Mayor, Mr. Irving, and Mr. Lowell. It seems to me that in every possible way all the proprieties and all the unities have attended it. It seems to be a graceful offering, modest, unobtrusive, unheralded, accepted in the spirit in which it is given. I wish MR. CHILDS might have been present here to-day. I wish he might have observed for himself the spirit in which his gift was received. It is appropriately erected on the place where the memory of Shakspeare has extinguished all other memories, a place to which Americans, by the pilgrimage of successive generations, have established a title as tenants in common with Englishmen by right of possession—one of those possessions described by Mr. Lowell, not laid down on the map, but of which the title is just as strong as if it were marked by geographical boundaries. I have sometimes thought that there is no bond of union between Americans and Englishmen that is stronger than that of a common literature; I mean the literature that pervades and influences the general intelligence of the country; the literature that was so ably portrayed by Mr. Irving this morning in his observations on the character of Shakspeare's writings; a literature which is not the property of a class, but for all mankind and for all time ; and therefore this birthplace of Shakspeare, where almost all the memorials which remain to him are gradually being gathered together, here, if anywhere in England, is the appropriate place for a permanent gift from an American. It is appropriate also in the time of offering, the Jubilee Year of your Sovereign—the Jubilee of which I was a most interested spectator in all its progress from beginning to end. And the impression which it made upon me was that its success and its distinction did not arise from its pageantry or its ceremonies or the distinguished concourse which attended it from afar. It has been in the manifestation of that deep and universal loyalty of this people towards their Queen and their Government. That, as it appears to me, is the lesson, the significance, the glory, and the success of the Jubilee. The loyalty of Americans is to their own Government; they appreciate the loyalty of your people to yours, and they understand and feel, I am sure, through the whole length and breadth of that country, what was so well expressed by the Mayor when he said that the throne of the Queen is in the hearts of her people. And therefore a gift which, though it comes from one citizen only in America, which will be applauded by thousands, and to which thousands would have gladly contributed if it had been requisite, may well come in the year **when** you are celebrating an event so rare in the history **of** nations. The gift, too, in its inauguration has been fortunate in the ceremonies that attended it. It is fortunate that it should have been inaugurated in an address so fitting and so elegant by a gentleman who interprets Shakspeare to both the nations in **whom** we claim a share and always shall, whom we always welcome heartily, and always unwillingly let go. I cannot wish him a speedy return, in justice to my countrymen, in the voyage he is about to undertake. I hope he may have a safe and happy one. I hope that, when the curtain falls in America upon some representation of the great Master which has entranced a theatre crowded with the best intelligence of my countrymen, and when the call not unfamiliar to his ear compels him to say something for himself, he will tell them what he has seen and heard to-day. He may be too modest to tell them how much he has contributed to it; but, I hope, he will tell them something of the manner and the spirit in which the gift to his country was received, and I am sure it will not make his welcome the less cordial. Long may this fountain stand, sir, and flow, an emblem, a monument, a landmark—not the only one by many, I hope—of the permanent, intimate, cordial friendship of my countrymen and yours! May many generations of Englishmen and Americans drink together of its waters! May many a schoolboy, creeping unwillingly to school, or rushing joyously away from it, when he pauses to slake his thirst at its current, take in with the water a kindly thought of his kinsmen beyond the sea—kinsmen who have so much in common, whose history, whose religion, whose literature, whose language are all in common, and who are to share in common hereafter, beyond all and above all, in that limitless American future which opens its magnificent doors free and wide to you and your children as well as to ours!'

A MESSAGE FROM THE QUEEN.

"At the conclusion of the address of the American Minister, which was received with the most enthusiastic manifestation of good-will, the Mayor announced, amid great cheering, that he had just received a telegram from her Majesty. It was as follows:—

"'The Queen is much gratified by the kind and loyal expressions contained in your telegram, and is pleased to hear of the handsome gift from Mr. Childs to Stratford-upon-Avon.

"'(Signed) HENRY PONSONBY.'

"It may be stated that a few minutes earlier the Mayor had wired :—

"'To Sir Henry Ponsonby, Balmoral Castle.

"'The toast of her Majesty's health most enthusiastically received on the occasion of the inauguration of the drinking fountain by Mr. Childs, a distinguished citizen of Philadelphia.

"'(Signed) ARTHUR HODGSON, Mayor of Stratford.'

TO THE MEMORY OF THE POET.

"Sir Theodore Martin, K. C. B., submitted 'The Immortal Memory of Shakspeare.' In what words, he asked, should he present to such an assembly and on such an occasion such a toast? Wordsworth spoke and most folk knew something of the thoughts 'that do often lie too deep for tears;' but a toast to the immortal memory of Shakspeare awakened thoughts which indeed lay far too deep for words. What language, however copious, however eloquent, was adequate to express what they as individuals, what the whole civilized world, owed to him who was 'not of an age, but for all time.' With a prodigality and a genius for which literature furnished no parallel, he poured forth play after play in which his poetic pen turned to shape and his imagination inspired with warm breathing life, and presented, under aspects and conditions as diversified as life itself, a multitude of ideal beings who yet were human to the core. Boundless treasures of thought and of imagination, the most exquisite charms of expression and of poetic beauty, illumined his pages; and even were they to throw out of account his poems and his sonnets, priceless as these were, some three or four of his plays would, alone, suffice to make a transcendent reputation. But when they passed in review the whole thirty-seven which the care of his brother actors had preserved for us, what must they think? He said the care of his brother actors, and not his own, and this should ever be remembered, for among the many marvels that surround the name of Shakspeare, not the least marvel of all, perhaps, was the apparent absence of all precaution on his part that the masterpieces of his genius should not be lost or fall into oblivion. But a gift so priceless, so divine, was not to be lost to mankind. The seeds of immortality were there from the first. He obtained a strong hold upon the best minds of his time. Steadily and surely his fame expanded with the widening culture of his countrymen, and as time rolled on, other lands, one by one, came to feel that in grasp and development of human character, in constructive skill, in breaks of genial humor, in intellectual force and wealth, Shakspeare towered alone. His fame and influence were now as wide as the civilized world, and the eyes of the nations turned with gratitude and reverence to the spot where first he saw the light, and to which he returned in the mellow and modest evening of his days. England had many memories to be proud of, but of none of her sons might she be prouder than of Shakspeare. What he now asked them to do would be done in many a land from time to time through many ages yet to come—ay! was it, even, too much to say until 'this great globe itself, and all that it inhabit, shall dissolve'?—he asked them now to drink with him to the immortal memory of Shakspeare.

"The toast was drunk in reverent silence.

THE TRIBUTE OF THE PRESS.

"Mr. Walter, the proprietor of the London 'Times,' proposed the next toast, which he said might truly be described as the toast of the day, the health of the honored donor of the gift which they had assembled to inaugurate. He had no claim whatever to be selected for so high an honor as that of proposing Mr. Childs's health, except from the circumstance that he had had the privilege of being intimately acquainted with Mr. Childs for more than twenty years, and that he and his family had, when visiting the United States, received unbounded proofs of his hospitality and affectionate feeling towards them, which had always made him (Mr. Walter) feel when within the States as a free citizen of that community. Only those who had had the good fortune to know America intimately could form any adequate idea of the feelings of veneration and attachment which most educated Americans entertained towards this country, and especially to those localities which were identified with noble, historic, and other glorious associations. And of all the counties of England, the county of Warwick, perhaps, from the historic associations connected with such places as Kenilworth, Warwick, and above all Stratford-upon-Avon, appealed most to the hearts of Americans, to make them feel that they were of one kindred and one race with ourselves. Sometimes, indeed, it had happened that the feeling had manifested itself in a somewhat extraordinary and not altogether acceptable manner. He remembered one instance of this which brought to his mind the feeling which Henry V. expressed towards Catherine when he said that he loved France so well that he would keep it all to himself. About thirty years ago —it might be more; it was when he was a young man —it occurred to an enterprising American that there was not sufficient feeling in Stratford-upon-Avon towards the memory of her immortal poet, and that it would be far better for the good, at all events of America, if the Americans put in practice the art for which they were known to be so eminently distinguished—the art of transplanting houses. It actually occurred to an enterprising dweller in the States to purchase and remove to America Shakspeare's house. Whether or not this was intended as a scare to compel that which was afterwards done—the purchase and the public guardianship of that wonderful treasure—it was not for him to say, but the impression it made on his mind was perfectly fresh, and he had no doubt it was familiar to most Americans. It had produced beneficial results to them in making them more highly and more thoroughly appreciate the honor of being the custodians of Shakspeare's house.

A PORTRAIT OF MR. CHILDS.

"With regard to MR. CHILDS himself he must say a few words, though, as the American Minister had said, that was a subject on which there was little more to say. MR. CHILDS was probably personally unknown to most of those now present. He was a man with a very remarkable history—one of those examples of self-made men of which the American soil seemed to be prolific; men who, by an early career of great industry, energy, shrewdness, and perseverance, acquired large fortunes and employed them for the public good. MR. CHILDS began life in a very humble capacity, making what few dollars he could in the best way he could find to his hand. He became a publisher, and amassed in that business a considerable sum. But he was an instance of a man who, like the Mayor, instinctively obeyed the wise teaching of their great poet by remembering that 'there is a tide in the affairs of men which taken at the flood leads on to fortune.' He took his chance at the flood, and became the purchaser of the PUBLIC LEDGER, which he had made a most lucrative and highly honorable paper, and upon that he had built a fortune which had enabled him to perform those acts of public and private generosity and unbounded **hospitality** to all Englishmen who had the good fortune **to be** introduced to his acquaintance, and of which the occasion of their present gathering was one of the most conspicuous examples. The other day, in reading a book which Mr. Childs gave him many years ago—a remarkable book, by an American—he came across a passage which seemed to him singularly appropriate to the present occasion, **which** he hoped would be sufficient excuse for his quoting a couple of stanzas from it. The poet was apostro**phizing** Shakspeare, and said:—

> 'Deep in **the** West, as Independence moves,
>   His banners planting round the land he loves,
>   Where Nature sleeps in Eden's infant grace,
>   In Time's full hour shall spring a glorious race.
>   Thy name, thy verse, thy language shall they bear,
>   And deck for thee the vaulted temple there!
>
>   'Our Roman-hearted fathers broke
>   Thy parent empire's galling yoke;
>   But thou, harmonious master of the mind,
>   Around their sons a gentler chain shalt bind!
>   Once **more in** thee shall Albion's sceptre wave,
>   And what her Monarch lost **her** Monarch-bard shall save!'

THE GIVER OF THE FOUNTAIN.

"One word to give some idea of MR. CHILDS. At the present moment it was about a quarter past nine by Philadelphia time, and MR. CHILDS was sitting at his breakfast—a piece of dry bread and a cup of milk —and wondering what sort of a day it was going to be in England, and how the most interesting ceremony at Stratford was about to pass off, and possibly even thinking in what terms his own health might be proposed. The news would probably have reached him before he had drunk his last cup of milk. Now, if he had to describe the character of MR. CHILDS in a single word, he should do so in a word which was impressed upon his mind by very early associations, and which the Mayor would forgive him for mentioning on the present occasion. Fifty-eight years ago he knew a little boy at school, with rosy cheeks, genial, beaming countenance, and such delightful qualities of civility, good-humor, and readiness to oblige, that his schoolfellows applied to him the epithet of 'trump.' Most schoolboy epithets were not complimentary, and he had never known of the application of that particular epithet to any other boy than that one, whom he remembered as Trump Hodgson.

He had developed, in the course of his interesting history, into the Worshipful Mayor of Stratford-upon-Avon. The Mayor would excuse him for mentioning the circumstance, and not think he was guilty of wishing to infringe upon his monopoly of the title, but if he had to apply one epithet rather than another to MR. CHILDS he should say he was a trump. He was a man of guileless habits, unselfish disposition, a readiness to do good in any way, and who could not possibly do an ill turn to any one. They were all indebted to MR. CHILDS for having performed an act which would help to impress upon their minds more than anything else the duty they owed to preserve the memory of their immortal bard always fresh in their minds. He ardently wished the rising generation could be persuaded to read more and more of Shakspeare and less of the trash which they daily devoured. He commended to them the health of their distinguished absent friend, MR. CHILDS, and asked them, not only to drink to his present health, but also to wish him a long continuance of prosperity and happiness.

"The toast was drunk amid loud applause.

THE VOICE OF AN OLD FRIEND.

"Dr. Macaulay, who, as an old friend of Mr. CHILDS, was asked to reply in his behalf, said he had been told by many persons that this gift of Mr. CHILDS to Stratford was creating an impression in America perhaps even beyond the value of the gift. And why? For the same reason as in England, that it was regarded as a pledge of the good feeling between the two nations. At the present time there was a very unusual deputation in America—many members of Parliament, with others—having an interview with the President of the United States, trying to get from him a contract that there should be no more war between the two nations, and that every question in dispute should be submitted to arbitration. But Mr. Phelps had very wisely told them contracts were of no avail unless they were supported by public opinion, and he (Dr. Macaulay) was sure that nothing would do more to create the desired state of public opinion than this generous act of Mr. CHILDS. It was a happy thought, this gift to the town of Shakspeare in the Jubilee Year of Queen Victoria, and he believed it would strengthen public opinion and make any diplomatic arrangement the more easy by making the two peoples feel that they had a common origin, a common feeling, and a common sympathy in all things, and when England and America were joined there was good hope for the security of the freedom and progress of the civilized world.

HENRY IRVING.

"Mr. C. E. Flower said he was sure that the Mayor had allotted to him a most pleasing as well as a most honorable duty in asking him to propose the health of their friend, Mr. Henry Irving. That morning they asked Mr. Irving to turn on the water; now he asked the company to turn on the wine in his honor. All in that room, everybody in Stratford, were delighted to welcome Mr. Irving. They were very grateful to him for having spared the time from his arduous duties and busy life to pay them a visit, and to take the part which he had so admirably fulfilled in the ceremony of that day. While they were pleased to welcome Mr. Irving, he thought he might also presume to say that he must be also pleased to come among them—pleased to have the honor of representing an old and valued American friend, and not the least gratified because that duty had brought him to the old town of Stratford. Mr. Irving, as most of them knew, had already some association and connection with Stratford. He had been from the first one of the governors of the Shakspeare Memorial Association, and only in the present year the trustees of the poet's birthplace had had the pleasure of electing him as one of their number. They had, in fact, endeavored to tie him to Stratford by bonds which, they hoped, he would not find irksome. While asking them to drink the health of Mr. Irving as an individual taking an important and responsible part in that day's ceremony, he was sure Mr. Irving would allow him to say that they also desired to drink his health as representing the profession of which he was so distinguished a member. There were many actors and actresses, living and passed away, who were held affectionately in the memory of Stratfordians, and he wished to propose the health of Mr. Irving who represented a profession which had done much of late years not only to enliven but to enlighten our social life. He therefore asked the company to drink the health of Mr. Irving, recognizing the great and honorable part he had played so well that day, remembering his associations with Stratford and its Shakspearian institutions, and greeting him as actor, gentleman, and friend.

"The toast was drunk with loud cheers.

AN AMBASSADOR TO MR. CHILDS.

"Mr. Irving, who, on rising to respond, was greeted with cheers again and again renewed, said : 'I thank you most heartily for your most kind welcome, and I reciprocate with all my heart your wishes that I may soon come to Stratford again, and may have the privilege of meeting many of the genial friends I have met here to-day. An actor can crave no higher distinction than that of being prominently associated with some public work in connection with Shakspeare's memory in Shakspeare's native town. It is the lasting honor of the actor's calling that the poet of all time was a player, and that he achieved immortality by writing for the stage. Of all the eloquent tributes which have been paid to Shakspeare one ever recalls the words of his fellow-actors, to whose loving care we owe the first edition of his works, and who tell us that "as he was a happy imitator of Nature, he was a most gentle expresser of it." All we can desire in the artistic embodiment of life this "most gentle expresser of Nature" has given us. I would like to quote a few words on this subject which seem to me to embrace a very great deal—a few words written by your Excellency's famous countryman Emerson, in which he pays Shakspeare a tribute which it would be very difficult to excel. He says: "We can discern, by his ample pictures of the gentleman and the king, what forms and humanities pleased him; his delight in troops of friends, in large hospitality, in cheerful giving. Let Timon, let Warwick, let Antonio the merchant answer for his great heart. So far from Shakspeare being the least known, he is the one person in all modern history known to us. What point of morals, of manners, of economy, of philosophy, of religion, of taste, of the conduct of life, has he not settled? What mystery has he not signified his knowledge of? What offices, or functions, or district of man's work has he not remembered? What king has he not taught state, as Talma taught Napoleon? What maiden has not found him finer than her delicacy? What lover has he not outloved? What sage has he not outseen? What gentleman has he not instructed in the rudeness of his behavior?" These are things which the actor treasures to the full as dearly as the student, and the actor's art to-day comes much nearer Shakspeare's estimate of its importance in the intellectual life of the community than in the times when the corporation of Stratford refused to permit the performance of Shakspeare's plays. I don't intend that reminder to touch any tender spot in your municipal pride now, for the players were not treated with contumely in Stratford at all, and perhaps it was the influence of Shakspeare's memory which induced the corporation on one occasion to pay them the handsome sum of forty shillings to keep away. But times are better now, and I am quite sure that when a troop of Lyceum players come to Stratford they will settle down under the wing of the Worshipful Mayor. In a few days I shall sail for the great country where any worthy representation of Shakspeare on the stage commands as staunch support from the public as in our own, and I cannot help thanking Mr. Phelps for his most genial words, which represent the more than cordial—I may say affectionate—welcome which we have always received from his countrymen. I shall act as your ambassador to MR. CHILDS, and I hope that in the course of the next fortnight I may convey to him your enthusiastic appreciation of his generous gift. I shall remember, Mr. Walter, your kind wishes and the affectionate tribute you have paid him, and I shall be the happy person to convey, I hope, to him my impressions of to-day. The ceremonial of to-day must have given the greatest pleasure to all, for it has renewed our hallowed associations with the mighty dead, and it has reminded two great nations of a bond which no calamity can dissolve. And, believe me, I am sure it will make every English-speaking actor in the world prouder than ever of the calling which I have the privilege of representing here to-day.'

A WORTHY CITIZEN.

"Mr. Samuel Timmins proposed the health of 'The Mayor.' Happily it was a text which required no sermon; and even what he might have said had been already anticipated in the interesting and admirable speech of Mr. Walter, referring to the school-boy days of his Worship. He really felt that there was nothing for him to add. So far as his memory served, Shakspeare was never very respectful to mayors, and he was certainly very disrespectful to town clerks on more than one occasion; but he was sure that, if Shakspeare were alive now, and had witnessed that day's ceremonies, he would have joined very heartily in drinking the toast which he had the honor to propose. He knew something of the history of the Mayor, and he had rarely met with a more remarkable example of industry, kindness, and generosity, leading to a high and honored place. The Mayor was entitled to the compliment of the toast, not only because of his share in the day's proceedings, but also because of his services to the town. Unlike Shakspeare, he had not the honor of being born in Stratford. That, of course, he could not help, and he was quite sure he regretted it, but he had made the best atonement in his power by coming to live in the neighborhood, and taking an active and successful part in the affairs of the town. In this he had followed Shakspeare's example. He was not aware that the Mayor had written a tragedy, or perpetrated a poem, or scribbled a sonnet; but he had certainly followed Shakspeare's example in a direction which it was difficult to understand nowadays, that after a highly successful and honorable career he had come down to a quiet little country but historic town and taken his lot and part in its good government and true advancement. Shakspeare did this, and the Mayor had done it, and that his services were appreciated was shown by the fact that he had been for four years the Mayor of the borough. Sir Arthur Hodgson was respected by his fellow-citizens, honored by all; and they had special reason to drink his health that day because he had been a very active and energetic supporter of the admirable proposal of Dr. Macaulay, through the generous donor, MR. CHILDS, that a drinking fountain should be erected in this town. For many years he had known the Mayor personally, as one of the trustees of the Birthplace, and he had always been struck with his ability, courtesy, and kindness. They desired to thank Sir Arthur for his generous, his princely—he would rather say, Mayoral—hospitality. Further, he had conducted the whole proceedings of that day with admirable taste and skill. He was sure the Mayor deserved that they should heartily drink the toast as a worthy citizen of whom Stratford, and even Shakspeare, might be proud.

"The company then separated.

MR. CHILDS'S THANKS TO SIR ARTHUR HODGSON.

"The Mayor, in the course of the afternoon, received the following telegram from the donor of the fountain:—

"'PHILADELPHIA.

"'To Sir Arthur Hodgson:

"You have my warmest thanks for the enlightened attention you gave to everything relating to the Shakspeare Fountain, and its successful dedication, which is a personal courtesy superadded to the official duty so well performed, and which it was certainly very gracious in you to bestow.

"'GEORGE W. CHILDS.'

TO A FRIEND BEYOND THE SEA.

"The following poem, written by Mrs. R. S. de C. Laffan on the opening of the fountain, was read by Mr. Henry Irving to the company assembled at Avon Bank on the eve of the ceremony:—

'Brothers yet—though ocean sever
    Your free land that fronts the west
From the churchyard by the river,
    Where our common fathers rest:

'Brothers—by the twin rills flowing
    From one fount of English speech,
By the common mem'ries glowing
    Deep within the heart of each:

"'It is yours, as it is ours,
   This most favored spot of earth,
 Where the springtime crowned with fowers
   Gave our gentle Shakspeare birth.

'Here, where every stone reminds us
   Of the name that each reveres,
 Symbol of the love that binds us,
   Changeless through the changing years,

'Rear the fountain: let the chiming
   Of its peal of silver bells
 Thrill like some sweet singer's rhyming
   Every heart in Avon's dells.

'Let its waters, softly plashing,
   Woo the weary and the worn,
 Brightly through the gloaming flashing,
   Brightly through the summer morn.

'So the wanderer onward pressing,
   Thirsty, way-worn, weak of knee,
 Halting here shall drink a blessing
   To a Friend beyond the Sea.'"

THE LONDON TIMES'S REPORT.

The London 'Times,' on the day following October 18, published an account of the dedication ceremonies, including the poem of Dr. Holmes, the addresses and letters above given, filling four of its broad, long columns, which it prefaced as follows under the caption of "Shakspeare and America :"—

"For all English-speaking people there is a peculiar and almost romantic charm about the town in which the opening and closing scenes in the life of Shakspeare were enacted. So inseparably, indeed, are most of the scanty personal records of the poet associated with Stratford-upon-Avon that the place itself has long since been invested with a character not far removed from that attaching to the shrine of a saint in the Middle Ages. Thousands of pilgrims annually resort to the quaint little midland town to examine with an interest akin to reverence the relics it contains, to look on scenes which must have been familiar to the poet, and to stand on the ground for ever sacred to his name and memory. Since the days of Washington Irving, American faces have been as numerous in Stratford as those of English people, and a handsome Memorial Window in the church where Shakspeare's dust reposes bears testimony to American appreciation of the poet and his work. Another evidence of transatlantic veneration for the memory of Shakspeare was seen yesterday at Stratford. This time the Memorial has assumed the form of a public drinking fountain and clock tower, which an American citizen, MR. GEORGE W. CHILDS, of Philadelphia, has presented to the town. The ceremony connected with the dedication of this new monument was one which can hardly fail to be of general and almost world-wide interest. The representative company which had assembled to witness the event, together with the international character of the gift itself, conspired to lend a more than ordinary importance to the proceedings on this occasion. Yesterday was warm and sunny, and nothing more appropriate than the bright October weather could have been desired for the performance of such a ceremonial. There are few English towns more prettily situated than Stratford-upon-Avon, and at this season of the year the charm is heightened by the beauty of the foliage. The flush of autumn still lingers on the valley of the Avon, and the views to be obtained from the old bridge and from the parish church are rendered more picturesque than ever by the mellow tints upon the landscape.

"The memorial has been erected in what is known as Rother Street, a broad, open space near the centre of the town, where several thoroughfares converge. It is here that the annual 'mops' or statute fairs take place, and the spot is admirably adapted for the site of the memorial. The structure is a handsome and imposing one.

"The ceremony of inaugurating the fountain was performed yesterday at noon by Mr. Henry Irving, in the presence of the Mayor of Stratford-upon-Avon (Sir Arthur Hodgson, K.C.M.G.), the Corporation, and a very numerous assemblage of visitors and townspeople. Among others present were Lord De La Warr, Mr. Phelps, the American Minister, Lord Ronald Gower, Sir Theodore Martin, Sir P. Cunliffe Owen, **Mr. John** Walter, Dr. Macaulay, Mr. J. C. Parkinson, Mr. Frank Marshall, and the Mayors of Lichfield, Coventry, Warwick, and Leamington. In the main streets of Stratford the Union Jack and the Stars and Stripes were conspicuously displayed, and the town wore an air of festivity and gayety throughout the day.

"At noon the Mayor and Corporation arrived in procession at the memorial."

THE LONDON 'DAILY TELEGRAPH'S' REPORT.

On the same day the London 'Daily Telegraph' published an account of the celebration as extended as that of the 'Times,' with the following introduction:—

"Stratford-upon-Avon—supremely lovely at all times; hallowed with its immortal memory of Shakspeare; consecrated to literary men and all lovers of the stage by anniversaries, and jubilees, and kindly ceremonies without number—was never lovelier than on the sunny October morning when, under the happy auspices of sunshine and good-fellowship, the leading actor of England dedicated, inaugurated, and consecrated the gift of an American citizen to the home and the birthplace of the poet of all time. All the hospitable houses in the neighborhood were full of distinguished guests. The genial and popular Mayor, Sir Arthur Hodgson, had invited his Excellency the American Minister, who appeared not in any diplomatic capacity, but as the mouthpiece and representative of his fellow-countryman, MR. GEORGE W. CHILDS, of Philadelphia, whose handsome present of a drinking fountain now stands unveiled and flowing with fresh water in the old Rother Market, and Sir Theodore Martin, who was selected to propose in his own graceful and felicitous manner the solemn toast of the 'Immortal Memory of Shakspeare.' Dr. Macaulay, who suggested the happy thought of the drinking fountain to his friend,

Mr. Childs, as well as Mr. Henry Irving, who was the hero of the hour and cheered whenever he was seen in Stratford, was hospitably entertained by Mr. Charles Flower, of Avonbank, who, with his brother, Mr. Edgar Flower, has done so much and worked so indefatigably and loyally in the cause of Shakspearian tradition, thinking, rightly and enthusiastically as they do, that Shakspeare's memory is a solemn legacy to the townsfolk of Stratford-upon-Avon. On this occasion Mr. Irving necessarily paid a flying visit to the good old town, which recognizes him as something more than a casual friend since he has been recently elected one of the trustees of Shakspeare's birthplace in Henley Street. As Mr. Irving was acting in Liverpool on Saturday, and has to sail for America on Thursday, his visit was necessarily brief, but his welcome none the less cordial and enthusiastic. Sunday was a glorious day—a little chilly, perhaps, in the teeth of the wind—but a bright sun lit up the glorious autumnal foliage, and the chance visitor to the good old town was continually running up against some one of note who has identified himself with Shakspearian literature, or has shown his personal enthusiasm for the place of Shakspeare's birth and death. In the beautiful old collegiate church, already in a fair way of restoration and free from its hideous and disfiguring galleries, that popular and enthusiastic Freemason, Mr. J. C. Parkinson, who some years ago rescued the archives of Stratford Masonry from destruction, and, having re-established the Stratford-upon-Avon lodge of Masons in the neighborhood of London, caused an entablature to be placed under the Freemason's window in the chancel, close by Shakspeare's grave, might have been seen looking after the interests of his craft, who hold Shakspeare's memory in such veneration. At Anne Hathaway's cottage, among the Michaelmas daisies and orange marigolds, Mr. Frank Marshall, the co-editor with Mr. Irving of the promised beautiful edition of Shakspearian acting plays, might have been found admiring the old settle and examining the fine-spun linen of the Hathaway family on the Shakspeare bed. Hovering about the Shakspeare house was the indefatigable Mr. Samuel Timmins, of Birmingham, an enthusiastic Shakspearian scholar; whilst it was impossible to take a walk that lovely day towards Charlecote or Clopton without meeting some one who has made some sort of name in literature or art.

"And then, of course, there was the imposing new fountain, the immediate object of attention to the countless pilgrims, the beautiful and costly gift of MR. CHILDS; the monument all pinnacles and stone tracery, the handsome combination of drinking-trough and clock-tower that stood uncovered in the bright October sunshine, attracting innumerable visitors to admire its proportions, **to** discuss its style of architecture, and to read the Shakspeare texts engraved on every available panel.

ON AVON'S BANK.

"Monday broke over Stratford even warmer, sunnier, and more genial than the day before, and at a very early hour the visitors scattered about in various directions. The greater part naturally betook themselves to the Shakspeare Memorial Buildings, on the Avon bank, already mellowing down with age, and containing the fruit of the anxious and devoted labors of the Flower family and their friends. The handsome and insulated theatre, standing at the lovely bend of the silent river close to the old church, is now supplemented by a library and a picture gallery of ample proportions, and additions to both are earnestly asked by those who have by degrees made the old town one of the show-places of

England, and directed thither the footsteps of countless American pilgrims, who recite Washington Irving in the cosy parlors of the celebrated Red Horse, and quote Shakspeare in the busy marketplace or the quiet churchyard. There was clearly much to be done before midday arrived, the hour fixed for dedicating Mr. Childs's fountain to the use and benefit of Shakspeare's native home. No one, for instance, could neglect to pay a visit to the old house in Henley Street, which Mr. Walter, in the course of the day, pleasantly reminded us was, once upon a time, threatened with annihilation by an enterprising American, who proposed to carry it bodily away and transplant it on the other side of the Atlantic. The old custodian's bell at the Shakspeare House was constantly set ringing, and those charming and courteous ladies, the Miss Chattaways, were continually repeating the well-known lecture in the same pleasant and cheerful terms.

"Shortly before mid-day a procession was formed at the Town Hall, headed by Sir Arthur Hodgson, K. C. M. G., the Mayor of Stratford, who was preceded by the beadle and macebearers of the ancient corporation, and followed by the Mayors of Worcester, Lichfield, Coventry, Warwick, Leamington, the Earl De La Warr, Mr. Phelps, the American Minister, Sir Theodore Martin, Sir Philip Cunliffe Owen, Lord Ronald Gower, Mr. Henry Irving, Mr. J. C. Parkinson, Dr. Macaulay, Mr. Timmins, Mr. Walter, of Bearwood, the vicar of Stratford, the Rev. de Courcy Laffan, and the ministers of every religious denomination in the town. There was only one sad disappointment. The worthy Mayor had received a letter from Mr. James Russell Lowell regretting his inability to be present, and the letter of apology was so eloquent that he did not hesitate to read it to the assembled people at the commencement of the ceremony."

Succeeding this was a report of the imposing ceremony, the poem, letters and addresses, and on the editorial page of the 'Telegraph' there appeared the accompanying striking leading article, the style of which will readily be recognized as that of the great Oriental scholar and poet whose genius has borne from the Englishmen's far East to all English-speaking peoples the poetry of those elder races of men who spoke in strange tongues with reverent love of all that was beautiful and tender in their religious faith. Through that sublime poem, 'The Light of Asia,' Sir Edwin Arnold has given to the peoples of a later civilization and creeds a poetic epitome of those ancient beliefs which foreran all modern ones.

SIR EDWIN ARNOLD'S TRIBUTE.

"To commemorate, or to celebrate, or in any way seek to magnify," said the learned and brilliant editor of the 'Daily Telegraph,' "the great name of Shakspeare is in a certain sense, of course, impossible. He is one of the very few among the immortals of our race who live beyond praise. The language which he enriched with deathless creations, and which his works rendered adequate to the majesty of this Empire, is a perpetual memorial of him. The land of which he was the glory and ornament is, in its length and breadth, his monument. He has passed beyond criticisms, to be studied, revered, cherished, and wondered at, as an inexhaustible source of delight, instruction, and deep lessons of humanity. The better qualified any person is to judge of masterpieces in literature; the more he may happen to know of the grandest works of Greek and Latin, of Oriental or mediæval writings, or of the finest achievements in our own tongue, the completer will be the pleasure with which he turns back again to the magic pages of Shakspeare or follows the track of his all-powerful genius in a well-acted representation. He cannot be exhausted, resembling in this respect the sublimest production of Nature herself. Admirers of his genius are perpetually endeavoring to glean something novel about his life and character; but we shall probably never know very much more about these than his own lordly carelessness has deigned to reveal. If even we did know more, it would not be elucidatory of the ultimate inspirations of so marvellous a man. All the folly talked about the mythical existence of William Shakspeare, of a cryptograph lurking in his sonnets and plays which indicates Lord Bacon or somebody else as their author, may be dismissed as rubbish. To any mind at all competent to arbitrate, the signet of an ineffaceable and intensely individual genius is visibly stamped upon every line of his work—nay, the very words are too felicitous to imagine altered. It is enough that we possess the simple facts which assure us of the general current and career of his life; that we know about his father, the woolstapler; of his birth in the little sacred street-house at Stratford-upon-Avon; of his love for Anne Hathaway, and his suit in the county court about a four-post bedstead; of his doings at the Globe, his lively ways, the look of his countenance, and the place of his interment. How it was that he understood everything without learning, and could think forth from every man's and woman's heart with its own feelings; how he could be—as he is—more majestic than an Emperor, more delicate than a maiden, wiser than a sage, courtlier than a noble, tenderer than any lover, and prouder than any conqueror, is a mystery which human wit cannot solve. It suffices that he was given to this realm, our immortal pride and heritage; that in one age and from one brain his single faculty established our common language as for ever classical and consecrated. It is Shakspeare who celebrates and commemorates England, not Englishmen Shakspeare; but he also belongs to all English-speaking people, and in such a spirit the ceremony of yesterday took place at Stratford-upon-Avon, and had its true and very significant interest.

A HAPPY EMBLEM.

"The handsome fountain and clock-tower just erected in Shakspeare's town, and inaugurated by Mr. Henry Irving, are the gift of an American citizen, MR. GEORGE W. CHILDS, of Philadelphia, well known already in his own country for an enlightened mind and munificent deeds. Such a tribute to the memory of the greatest of English poets is one that can be heartily hailed, and for which, in this Jubilee Year of our Queen, there was place and propriety. Equally appropriate it was that the dedication of this graceful gift to the town of Stratford should have been made by the first among living interpreters of the text of Shakspeare upon the stage. No actor would dispute this title with the accomplished and scholarly gentleman who has done so much to revive popular delight in the works of the Chief of Dramatists, and by this and other examples has so notably elevated the status of his profession. In the excellent speech which Mr. Irving delivered at the foot of the 'Jubilee Memorial,' he touched the central point of the ceremony at once by remarking that in that spot, of all spots, Americans and Englishmen ceased to be other than fellow-countrymen. We might, **indeed,** almost call Stratford-upon-Avon the joint capital of the British England and of the American England, as the Greeks looked upon Delphi as the true centre of the habitable globe. American life and literature, as Mr. Irving remarked, are as much stamped with the influence of the Bard of Avon as are our own; and it is at once the most satisfactory and the most natural thing in the world that **half** the names of the visitors inscribed in the book kept at the 'historic cottage' should have after them 'those imposing letters, U. S. A.' We rejoice to think that every American beyond the Atlantic longs to visit the birthplace of Shakspeare, and almost every one who comes over to our shores goes thither first of all if he can. They are quite right. Shakspeare belongs to them as much as to us, and the fountain of Mr. Childs is an impressive and acceptable way of emphasizing their sense of property in the memorable name. Nor was Mr. Irving otherwise than happily inspired in praising the character of the gift to the little town. It is simple, natural, homely, and for universal use—is a fountain —like the genius of the poet. As he remarked, 'Learned and unlearned, gentle and humble, may all alike drink from it; and so it seems to me,' said the speaker, 'that no happier emblem of Shakspeare's work in his native place could have been chosen.' Possibly we English might have been a little jealous if Mr. Childs had proposed to erect by the silver Avon a colossal statue, or a prodigious pyramid, or something which would have made British devotion look small; but the fountain and clock-tower are as becoming as they are significant of the feelings so delightfully conveyed in the letter of Mr. James Russell Lowell. 'I am glad to think,' he wrote, 'that this memorial should be the gift of an American, and thus serve to recall the kindred blood of the two great nations, joint heirs of the same noble language and of the genius that has given it a cosmopolitan significance. I am glad of it, because it is one of the multiplying signs that those two nations are beginning to think more and more of the things in which they sympathize, less and less of those in which they differ.'

A PEACE-OFFERING.

"Thus, then, even from his ashes our **great** Englishman renders us all a splendid new service, drawing closer together those portions of the English-speaking race which must never again be enemies. The key-note which had been so well and justly struck by Mr. Irving and taken up by Mr. James Russell Lowell was harmoniously utilized by the American Minister, who in a most genial and friendly speech said a great many happy and handsome things about our Queen, our country, and the relations between Englishmen and Americans. Mr. Phelps did, indeed, actually charge Mr. Henry Irving with a regular diplomatic mission, for he bade the universally popular actor not to lose an opportunity, the next time he was called upon for a speech before the curtain in the States, of relating what had been said and done at Stratford-upon-Avon in the inauguration of the CHILDS MEMORIAL. 'I am sure,' said the American Minister, 'it will not make his welcome less cordial; and long may this fountain stand and flow, an emblem, a monument, a landmark—not the only one by many, I trust—of the permanent, enduring, hearty, cordial friendship between my countrymen and yours! May many generations of Englishmen and Americans drink together of its waters!' After this deliberate choice of Mr. Irving as an ambassador of good-will between the two great nations, we ought almost to call him 'His Excellency' for the future. Moreover, that nothing might be wanting to grace the interesting occasion, her Majesty despatched a gracious telegram, saying with what pleasure she had heard of the sentiments prevailing at the gathering, and how glad she was to know of the handsome gift made to Shakspearians by MR. CHILDS. The generous donor himself was not able to be present, but the tidings which will reach him cannot fail to convey the conviction that he has done a useful as well as an enlightened and amicable act in thus establishing a monument of American loyalty to our poet on the soil of his birth and death. Nothing but good all round can result from so perfectly well-conceived a ceremony; nor could any words more fitly express this than those with which Mr. Irving closed his speech of thanks, observing: 'To-day's ceremonial has given infinite pleasure to all, for it has renewed our hallowed associations with the mighty dead, and it has reminded two great nations of a bond which no calamity can dissolve. And, believe me, it will make every actor in the world-wide sphere of Shakspeare's influence prouder than ever of the calling which I have the privilege of representing here.'"

OTHER BRITISH PRESS VIEWS.

In its issue of October 22 the London 'Graphic,' the illustrated rival of the 'News,' published a full-page drawing of the fountain taken during the celebration, in which were presented the attending multitude of participants, the portraits of many of them being given, together with an admirable likeness of

Mr. CHILDS. An extended description of the celebration accompanied this interesting sketch.

The London 'Globe' of the 18th of October contained the following introduction to an attractive account of the dedicatory ceremonies:—

"There was general rejoicing at Stratford-upon-Avon yesterday, the occasion being the inauguration of a splendid drinking fountain, which has been presented to the town as a Jubilee Memorial of the Queen's reign by MR. GEORGE W. CHILDS, of Philadelphia, the donor of the American Window in Westminster Abbey to the genius of Herbert and Cowper. The ancient borough accepted the gift with enthusiasm, and the Mayor and corporation issued invitations to one hundred guests. The American Minister (Mr. Phelps), Sir Philip Cunliffe Owen, Lord Ronald Gower, and Mr. John Walter were the guests of the Mayor, Sir Arthur Hodgson; Sir P. Cunliffe Owen, and Mr. Walter, proprietor of the 'Times,' being personal friends of MR. CHILDS. Mr. Henry Irving, who had accepted the task of making the dedication, was among the distinguished guests. The early trains brought the Lord Lieutenant of Warwickshire and the Mayors of the surrounding towns. The weather was beautifully fine, and the town was decorated with bunting. At half-past eleven o'clock the Mayor and the members of the corporation met at the Town Hall, and shortly before noon marched in procession to the site of the memorial, accompanied by Mr. Irving and the numerous representatives of literature, art, and the drama who had been invited. Mr. Irving, in making the dedication, spoke of MR. CHILDS as not only an admirable representative of the public spirit and enterprising energy of Philadelphia, **but** also as a man who had endeared himself to a very wide circle by many generous deeds. A letter was read from Mr. James Russell Lowell, and Sir P. Cunliffe **Owen** spoke as a friend of MR. CHILDS.

"A telegram was received from the Queen, in which Her Majesty stated that she was much gratified by the kind and loyal expressions conveyed, and was pleased to hear of the handsome gift by MR. CHILDS to Stratford-upon-Avon. Great cheering acknowledged the receipt of this telegram. Mr. Phelps's speech, in which he spoke of the loyal feeling towards the Queen entertained by Americans, was also received with loud cheers."

APPRECIATION.

The thorough and genuine appreciation of MR. CHILDS's gift **by** the English people **is** thus finely expressed by the Warwick 'Advertiser,' a journal of influence published near to the home of Shakspeare.

"The opening of the CHILDS MEMORIAL FOUNTAIN at Stratford-upon-Avon was an event of international importance. The spirit in which the gift was proffered and received will tend to cement the bond which unites us with our kinsmen beyond the sea in that great Republic of the West, which has such boundless possibilities in store for the Anglo-Saxon race."

The London 'Standard,' in a very full account of the celebration, said:—

"Mr. Irving inaugurated the monument, and had at his side several persons familiar to the public eye. During the proceedings a graceful message was received from the Queen, and from Mr. James Russell Lowell a letter was read congratulating England and America on the ever-growing sympathy of feeling and unity of opinion and sentiment between them. There is no more attractive place in the world than Stratford-upon-Avon for those who possess in any degree the 'mind's eye' spoken of by the Poet who has made it famous for all time. The little Warwickshire town is very pleasing in itself, even to the outward gaze, being kept scrupulously

clean, and neat, and comely by its denizens, who seem to be conscious of the privilege and responsibility they inherit by living there. Even for mere natural beauty of the quiet, smiling, and unsensationally charming order, few bits of scenery can surpass the short reach of the river that lies between lock and lock, at the upper end of which stands the Church, with its solemn cincture of graves and green girdle of trees, in which rest Shakspeare's 'honored bones.' There is an air of tranquil self-respect about Stratford-upon-Avon, as though the place were aware of its own dignity. Its outskirts **are** equally attractive and sanctified by vague **but** assured memories. What is more English than the path through the meadows along the river side, where now and then an otter disports himself?—and nowhere in the world is there a homelier, more dreamy, and more suggestive spot than Anne Hathaway's Cottage. There is no fear of Stratford-upon-Avon being forgotten, or of the birthplace and burial-place of Shakspeare losing its magic. The fear rather is that it should draw to itself too many pilgrims, as, indeed, even now it occasionally does. Every year is a Jubilee Year as far as Shakspeare's memory and fame are concerned, and nothing more can be done **to** extend his glory or to extol his genius. His is the one genius, in post-classical literature, that is beyond challenge, and provokes no controversy. In genius—that is to say, in depth, height, breadth, and variety of imagination, conception, and execution—he stands alone. All other writers, compared with him, belong to the second class. All men together can add nothing to, and **take** nothing away from, his reputation. It is well that Stratford-upon-Avon should have its Fountain and its Clock; and it is well, again, that they should be given by one of our and his kindred across the Atlantic. But they serve to shed no fresh **light** and no fresh lustre on the greatest of all names **in** the glorious Roll of Letters."

To the foregoing was added, in a leading editorial article:—

"All Englishmen will echo the friendly and just language of the American Minister, who was pres**ent,** and of **Mr.** James Russell Lowell, to whose letter we have referred. Indeed, an Englishman must be hopelessly insular who can think of a citizen of the United States as a stranger, much more as a foreigner; and an American must be deeply affected with spread-eagleism who looks on England as other than his parent country. It is interesting to note the exceeding eagerness of all refined and thoughtful Americans to strengthen the intellectual and historical link that already unites the two peoples on the two sides of the ocean. Our brethren on the other side of the sea have produced numbers of writers, and two or three poets whose charm all the world has recognized. But they have not produced—and they never are likely to produce—a Shakspeare. Theirs the future may possibly be, but the past is unquestionably ours. They are welcome to share it with us, and we could be glad to have a share in their future."

THE 'PALL MALL.'

In the issue of October 18, the London 'Pall Mall Gazette' published a very effective pictorial sketch of the fountain, accompanied by the following report of the ceremonies:—

"The handsome clock tower and fountain which Mr. CHILDS, of Philadelphia, has presented to the town of Stratford-upon-Avon, were inaugurated to-day by Mr. Henry Irving. It is fitting that a memorial to the greatest English dramatic poet should be inaugurated by that poet's greatest living interpreter on the stage. Mr. Irving is, moreover, a personal friend of the donor, MR. CHILDS, to whom in a few days he will carry the enthusiastic thanks of the town for his generous gift. Mr. Phelps, the American Minister, and Mr. James Russell Lowell have accepted invitations to the ceremony, and will speak at the banquet given by the Mayor.

"Mr. Irving arrived at Stratford by special train from London last night, and was most enthusiastically cheered on entering the town. Early trains this morning brought the Mayors of several surrounding towns. MR. CHILDS is in America, but he was represented by Dr. Macaulay, of 'The Leisure Hour,' and Sir Philip Cunliffe Owen. The weather was delightfully fine, and the town bore quite a gay appearance. At half-past eleven the Mayor and corporation went to the Town Hall, whence they proceeded to the memorial. Art, literature, and the drama were fully represented. Mr. Irving eulogized MR. CHILDS as being not only an admirable representative of the public spirit and enterprise of Philadelphia, but also as a man who had endeared himself to a very wide circle by many generous deeds. A letter was read from Mr. James Russell Lowell in which he said he was glad to find that the people of the two countries were thinking more of the things in which they agreed than of those in which they disagreed."

The editorial comment of the 'Gazette' was as follows :—

"It is not often that an inauguration goes off with such unclouded *éclat* as yesterday's function at Stratford-upon-Avon. The day was of October's best, and the ceremony was one of unique interest—the opening, namely, by the first actor in England, of the drinking fountain and clock tower which have just been erected in the Rother Market as a tribute by an American citizen to the genius of Shakspeare and to the virtues of Queen Victoria. MR. CHILDS makes the Jubilee Year the occasion of his gift. We gave yesterday a sketch of the fountain, which does great credit to the architect, Mr. Cossins, of Birmingham, and should bring him into notice for work of this description. But it was perhaps not so much either the fountain, or its cost, or even the international character of the gift, which collected from all parts of England the distinguished company which assembled yesterday in the Rother Market. Few Englishmen have travelled in America who have not, like Sir Philip C. Owen, Mr. Walter, and Dr. Macaulay, been acquainted with MR. CHILDS and enjoyed his sumptuous hospitality. He has been to them a sort of

British proxenos in Philadelphia, and it was a desire to testify their gratitude and friendship for a very lovable man which brought many to Stratford yesterday. There was, moreover, a certain appropriateness in the selection at the subsequent lunch of Mr. Walter, the owner of the London 'Times,' to propose the health of MR. CHILDS, the owner of the Philadelphia LEDGER. In their respective cities those two papers represent, and have now for many years represented in a remarkable degree, the sober traditions and stereotyped proprieties of long-established journalism. But if the 'Times' represents what is sober and solid, the LEDGER is the very essence of sobriety and solidity. It has never yet condescended to attract readers by the exhibition of posters; no map or plan, still less any portrait or engraving, has ever variegated the uniformity of its pages. Indeed, many people go so far as to say that the thousands of persons who peruse the LEDGER read it from pure affection and regard for MR. CHILDS. One of its most distinctive peculiarities is that it never says an ill word of any one, not even of a mother-in-law. But perhaps the real secret of MR. CHILDS's popularity is not so much his abstinence from ill words as the abundance of his good deeds. The Stratford fountain is one of many public benefactions, but his public benefactions, as any one acquainted with Philadelphia will bear witness, are far outnumbered by a multitude of acts of private charity and kindness of which the public never hears at all. 'I intend,' said Mr. Childs to a friend on last New Year's day, 'to be kinder this year than ever I was before;' and the saying and the fact that he said it are very characteristic of Mr. Childs.

"It is, therefore, a subject of congratulation to no small circle of friends that the inauguration of the fountain went off so brilliantly. The Mayor, Sir Arthur Hodgson, K. C. M. G., looked and spoke the part worthily of a Mayor of Stratford. Mr. Irving, standing in the granite trough from which endless generations of Warwickshire horses will quench their thirst, pronounced a speech of such grace and literary refinement as was only equalled by his own graceful and refined appearance. He read, too, Dr. Oliver Wendell Holmes's verses with a beauty of utterance which would have forced the enthusiastic little doctor himself to join in the vociferous applause produced by the production of his own pen. Of Mr. Phelps it is enough to say that he spoke as well as Mr. Lowell himself could possibly have done; of Sir Theodore Martin, that he was eloquent and sonorous. As Mr. Lowell was not able to be present, he sent a letter, which was read by Sir Arthur Hodgson.

"Perhaps, however, of all said and written, the sentence that will last longest is one of those selected by Dr. Macaulay and engraved on the fountain, which, for appropriateness, was never surpassed and deserves to appear on other fountains: 'Honest water, which ne'er left man i' the mire.' ('Timon of Athens,' act 1, scene 2.) A bottle filled with this 'honest water,' and carefully sealed up, was delivered to Mr. Irving, and will be duly conveyed by him to America next Thursday for presentation to MR. CHILDS in Philadelphia."

THE CROWNING EVENT OF THE JUBILEE YEAR.

In its issue of October 18, the Birmingham 'Daily Post,' a journal which in character and influence is to England's provincial press what the London 'Times' is to metropolitan journalism, gave the subjoined introduction to an account of the memorial ceremony, which occupied the larger part of one of its spacious pages:—

"Stratford-upon-Avon arrayed herself in a festival garment of sunshine, yesterday, for a function which, if not quite, as the Mayor enthusiastically called it, 'the crowning event of the Jubilee Year,' was of striking internal and literary significance. Mr. Henry Irving inaugurated the memorial fountain and clock tower which MR. G. W. CHILDS, a citizen of Philadelphia, has presented to the town. The function was a singularly quiet one, as all functions in such an old-world place as Stratford must necessarily be; but it was not the less significant and interesting on that account. MR. CHILDS's beautiful gift is remarkable alike as a reverent tribute to the memory of Shakspeare from a distant member of the English-speaking race, and as a token of the good-will which subsists between the British and the American nations. Moreover, the little crowd which gathered to assist at the ceremony was representative in some degree of the whole race, of all the learned professions, and of all estates of the realm.

"Sir Arthur Hodgson, in his own person, carried the proceedings through with a fine fervor of enthusiasm which infected every one about him. The memorial itself must always command admiration. It stands alone in the centre of the old 'rother,' or cattle market—a graceful pile of white Peterhead stone, tapering by bold buttresses and pointed gablets to a pretty finial. It is adorned with tiny statues of some of Shakspeare's most fanciful creations—Puck, Mustard-seed, Peas-blossom, and Cobweb bringing the fruits which Bottom was facetiously pleased to ask for, and a host of other quaint, imagined beings, peering down from the mouldings. The ornament is emblematic of the union of the two nations, and the base **bears four** well-chosen inscriptions—one recording the gift; another embodying the prophecy which, occurring in the play of 'Henry VIII.,' seems to be so well fulfilled in the present reign; a third, in Washington Irving's words, crying 'ten thousand honors and blessings on the bard who has gilded the dull realities of life with innocent illusions;' **and** a fourth, over the drinking-cups, in praise of 'honest water, which ne'er left man i' the mire.' This is not the only gift of MR. CHILDS to the English people. He is the donor of the American Window in Westminster Abbey in memory of George Herbert and William Cowper, of which tribute Dean Stanley is said to have been especially proud, and for which he wrote an inscription. The munificent public spirit with which his name is associated has become possible for him as the result of a pushing and successful career as a journalist. His personality was yesterday sketched by a lifelong friend when Mr. Walter, of the 'Times,' described him to the luncheon party assembled to share the Mayor's hospitality at the Town Hall.

"Two circumstances joined to rob the day's doings of a portion of their pleasure. One was the absence of Mr. James Russell Lowell, whom Englishmen have learned to greet as a dear friend; the other was the necessity for hurrying through the programme in order that Mr. Irving might depart for London. But Mr. Lowell sent a letter of apology which served for a speech, and **Dr.** Oliver Wendell Holmes some rhythmic and scholarly verses, which were better than a speech; while Mr. Irving, all unasked, promised to bring over to the Memorial Theatre his Lyceum 'troop of players.' Besides, there was a gracious message from the Queen, expressing her pleasure at hearing of MR. CHILDS's handsome gift, and a characteristic letter from Mr. Whittier. Mr. Irving's speeches were marked by the depth of thought, the grace of expression, and the music of delivery which were to have been looked for from him; and he made quite a telling picture as he stood against the white fountain reading Dr. Holmes's stanzas, **his** fine face lighted up with the sentiment, and his iron-grey locks exposed to the sun. Mr. Phelps, who spoke only at the luncheon, exalted the occasion and all such friendly occasions at the expense of international treaties, as to which he had some straightforward things to say. The day was brightened by an incident which, though not a part of the official programme, was of a piece with all that went before and came after. The Vicar of Stratford made his peace with Mr. Samuel Timmins. He came forward at the fountain and shook hands with that gentleman, who returned his grasp with interest, and so a quarrel was **made up** which has excited a good deal of comment among all who take interest in Shakspeare's town. In the same happy way, the Memorial may be said to have atoned for the barbarous proposal of a certain commercial Yankee to buy up the poet's house and move it bodily to America, and for the ingenious attempt of one of his countrymen to show that Shakspeare could not write, but made his mark, like Bill Stumps.

"The ceremony at the fountain took place at noon, the Mayor and his guests having assembled at the Town Hall a few minutes previously. The procession to the Square was headed by the Snitterfield Brass Band, and the civic portion of it **was** preceded by the Sergeants-at-Mace and brought up by the Corporation Beadle. The Mayors of Stratford and of the neighboring boroughs, with other official personages, wore the robes and other insignia of their offices. The local corps of Volunteers, headed by their drum-and-fife band, had previously arrived, and had taken up their position as a guard of honor near the fountain."

THE JOINING OF HANDS.

In the same number of the 'Daily Post,' the following editorial comment was made :—

"Literature and **Art**, the Press and the **Stage**, England and America, joined hands yesterday at Stratford-upon-Avon, in doing honor to one of the most illustrious representatives of our common stock, and **in** doing so it is scarcely necessary to add that they did honor to themselves and contributed **in no** mean degree to draw closer the bonds of union between the great two branches of the English-speaking **race**. The memorial fountain **and** clock tower, which **were formally** presented to Shakspeare's native town on this occasion on behalf of **Mr. Childs**, the well-known newspaper proprietor **and** editor of Philadelphia, are not by any means the first tribute of the kind which has been offered up by American citizens at that beloved shrine, which is every year the Mecca for so many troops of reverent pilgrims from beyond the Atlantic; but Mr. Childs's gift possesses a special international significance from the expressed desire of the donor that it should be construed as a token of good-will towards us in this Year of the Jubilee, and should serve to cement the union of two great nations 'that have the fame and works of the poet Shakspeare as their common heritage.' **And that** nothing might be wanting to the completeness **of** yesterday's function, the dedication was graced by characteristic contributions from some of the **most** renowned men of letters in the great Republic of the West, including Mr. James Russell Lowell, the ex-American Minister; **Mr.** John Greenleaf Whittier, the venerable Quaker poet; and Dr. Oliver Wendell Holmes, whose poem, specially written for the occasion, so happily and eloquently expresses the aspirations **to** which the gift naturally lends itself. On the English side, the stage, which is under so deep and special a debt of gratitude to the great dramatist, was not unworthily represented **by** Mr. Irving, on whom devolved the proud task of inaugurating the memorial; whilst the English newspaper press, in the person of Mr. Walter, the chief proprietor of the 'Times', cordially acknowledged and welcomed this substantial token of goodwill from a brother journalist of the New World. Mr. Irving is always happy on occasions of this kind, in which the actor for a time plays out his role, or rather sinks the interests of the profession to which he belongs in the wider interests of the English citizen; and his little address yesterday was equally excellent in taste and felicitous in illustration—in none more so, perhaps, than in the passage where he pictures Shakspeare returning from his bourne 'to find upon the throne a Queen who ruled with gentler sway than the great sovereign he knew, and yet whose reign had glories more beneficent than those of Elizabeth.' But the palm for graceful felicity of thought and diction must be awarded to Mr. James Russell Lowell, whose letter is a model of its kind. It was Washington Irving, he reminds us, who first embodied in his delightful English the emotion which Stratford-upon-Avon awakes in the heart of the American pilgrim who visits it, and he rejoices that this international memorial, which recalls the kindred blood of two great nations, 'joint heirs of the same noble language and of the genius that has given it a cosmopolitan significance,' should be the gift of an American. He hails it as one of the multiplying signs that the two nations 'are beginning to think more and more of the things in which they sympathize, and less and less of those in which they differ.' The territorial interests which we once held in common are sundered, but the ties of blood and race survive, and are forcibly brought home to us as we join in common worship before the shrine of Shakspeare. These ties, we devoutly hope with Mr. Lowell, will be drawn closer as science goes on abolishing time and space, favoring that 'peaceful commerce 'twixt dividable shores' which is so potent to clear away 'whatever is exclusive in nationality or savors of barbarism in patriotism.' The Queen's message of congratulation was a happy thought, which cannot but assist the working of the charm; and the proceedings altogether were of an order to entitle the day to a red-letter mark in the calendar, not only of Stratford, but of England and the United States."

FRATERNAL RELATIONS.

On the same day the Liverpool 'Post,' another provincial journal of high character, prefaced the long and interesting report of the proceedings at Stratford with these appreciative remarks:—

"The fraternal relations of the two great nations which regard the works of Shakspeare as a common heritage were shown in a happy manner at Stratford-upon-Avon to-day. Some time ago a prominent and respected citizen of the United States, MR. GEORGE W. CHILDS, of Philadelphia, determined to celebrate the Jubilee Year of Queen Victoria's reign by a memorial of American sympathy to be erected in the birthplace of England's greatest poet. MR. CHILDS, it may be recollected, is the donor of the American Window placed in Westminster Abbey to the memory of George Herbert and William Cowper. MR. CHILDS's gift to Stratford has taken the form of a drinking fountain and clock tower, and their inauguration to-day was made the occasion of a ceremonial of international interest, forming both a welcome and substantial benefit to the town, and a graceful addition to its many points of natural and historic interest. Stratford accepted the bequest with a heartiness at once agreeable to its author, and illustrative of the friendly feeling of the Warwickshire people for those of the great Republic of the West. The Mayor of Stratford, Sir Arthur Hodgson, K.C.M.G., in accepting Mr. Childs's munificence, arranged for an inaugural ceremonial befitting its international as well as practical character. Sir Arthur issued invitations on a scale of imposing hospitality, and among the one hundred guests invited, most of whom sent responsive replies, were the Lord-Lieutenant of Warwickshire, Earl De La Warr, the Mayors of Birmingham, Warwick, Coventry, Leamington, Lichfield, and Worcester, the American Minister (Mr. Phelps), Sir Theodore Martin, Lord Ronald Gower, Mr. Henry Irving (one of the trustees of Shakspeare's birthplace), Dr. Macaulay (of 'The Leisure Hour'), Sir Philip Cunliffe Owen, Mr. J. C. Parkinson, Mr. John Walter of the 'Times,' and other Shakspearian scholars and representatives of literature, art, and the drama. The townsfolk themselves, seconding the efforts of the chief magistrate, decorated their houses with bunting, flowers, and evergreens, closing their places of business during the ceremonial, and exhilarating the sense of prevailing enthusiasm by the music of their excellent Volunteer Band. The interest of Stratford itself was shared also by the inhabitants of the neighboring districts. Stratford-upon-Avon typifies all that is rustic and interesting in a well-preserved English town. The most unemotional observer, moreover, is made quickly aware that he is in the birthplace of Shakspeare. There are memorials of the bard at nearly every corner. Shakspeare's name is found upon men and things, and one might forgive **the** local innkeeper if he gave the pilgrim a salutation in the language of the great dramatist, or in the manner of Mr. Irving, who has come to be himself a kind of twin patron saint of Stratford—a demigod, the only man next to the illustrious genius whose works he interprets. But, though the *menu* card used at the luncheon was ingeniously interspersed **with** cunningly appropriate mottoes culled from Shakspeare's masterpieces, the conductors and waiters of the two excellent hotels are content to execute their service in the language of latter-day prose. Neither is there reason to believe that the Chief Constable of the town dismisses his men to their duty with a charge modelled upon Dogberry's, or that the good watchmen themselves pass the night under the church porch, so that they may amiably suffer rogues and other unclean persons to steal incontinently out of their neighborhood."

KINDRED BLOOD.

Editorially the 'Post' referred to the memorial celebration in the words following:—

"A handsome memorial fountain and clock tower, presented by MR. G. W. CHILDS, of Philadelphia, to 'Shakspeare's town in the Jubilee Year of Queen Victoria,' were publicly inaugurated at Stratford-upon-Avon yesterday by Mr. Henry Irving. Among those present were Mr. Phelps, the American Minister. In handing over the memorial to the Mayor, Mr. Irving said he rejoiced in the happy inspiration which prompted a gift that so worthily represented the homage of two great peoples to the most famous man of their common race. A letter was read from Mr. James Russell Lowell, who wrote that the memorial would serve to recall the kindred blood of the two great nations—joint heirs of the same noble language, and of the genius that had given it cosmopolitan significance. During the proceedings the Mayor despatched a message to the Queen announcing that the toast of her Majesty's health had been most loyally received by the distinguished company present. Shortly afterwards, a reply was received from her Majesty stating that she was much gratified **by the loyal** and kind expressions contained in the Mayor's telegram, and interested to hear of the handsome gift of MR. CHILDS."

THE VOICE OF THE 'WORLD.'

The American newspaper press demonstrated, by the publication of special cable despatches, by letters from special correspondents, and by editorial expressions of approval and admiration, that the interest in and sympathy with **the spirit of MR. CHILDS's gift** were not less strong among the people of this country than among those of England. The despatches from Stratford to the New York 'World' filled four and a half of the long broad columns of that journal, of which the following abstract was made :—

"GEORGE W. CHILDS'S memorial to Shakspeare was inaugurated to-day with much imposing ceremony. Stratford-upon-Avon has never before held so many strangers within its walls as to-day. Hundreds of Americans ran down from London last night and by the early morning trains, taxing to the utmost the somewhat limited facilities of the quiet old town for harboring transient guests. The new Shakspeare House was packed with transatlantic pilgrims, and some amusement was created **by the** boniface shouting out, as the weary wayfarers arrived, 'Take this young couple up to Romeo and Juliet.' The chambers in the old inn bear the names of the works written by the immortal Will—or somebody **else.** A melancholy American tragedian, lately crushed by the English critics, seemed somewhat put out when shown up to 'Hamlet,' and an elderly couple from Chicago did not like their quarters in 'Love's Labor's Lost.' For the first time in two weeks, according to the local weather man, the sun shone in Stratford this morning, setting off the handsome gift of the philanthropic Philadelphian to its best advantage. From dawn until midday the roads from the surrounding country were thronged with every sort of vehicle, from the dog-cart of **the** gentry to the ox-team of the yokel. The local and neighboring dignitaries, bearing up proudly under their massive gold chains and other weighty insignia of office, strode through the broad streets lined with quaint old-fashioned houses, making a truly old-world picture. The Town Crier was much alarmed by the numbers, and told me quietly that 'some would have to go home hungry, and that "Lunnon" certainly must look deserted.' But everything went off without a hitch, and, best of all, none of the many

improvident pilgrims went home hungry, thanks to **the** municipal hospitality.

"When the time came Mayor Hodgson wound **up** the clock in the stone spire, and Henry Irving turned on **the** first flow of the precious liquid. But the arrival of the Queen's telegram was **the** sensation of the day, not being on the card and being quite unexpected. The telegraph operator rushed headlong from the office down to the square. Mr. Phelps's speech was interrupted, and the **precious** despatch was read. It was the first time that Stratford has heard from the Queen telegraphically for thirty-five years. Throughout the day the attending bands of music played, with absolute impartiality, 'God Save the Queen' and 'Hail Columbia,' while the citizens of Greater Britain beyond the seas sported miniature union jacks in their buttonholes, and the inhabitants of 'the tight little isle' were resplendent **in** stars and stripes.

"Graceful in its inception, the generous gift of MR. CHILDS was gracefully received, and the ceremonies concluded in the most graceful manner possible by a banquet, which was as excellent **in** the material way as had been the preceding flow of wit and wisdom. The Stratford folk do not seem to be imbued in the least with any belief in the Baconian theory. In fact, they look upon it as a base attempt to rob their town of one of its chief claims to revenue and repute, and regard it as being inspired by an invidious neighbor."

UNDER BRIGHTEST AUSPICES.

Another of the 'World's' special correspondents added this introduction to a very comprehensive report of the entire presentation ceremonies:—

"The inauguration of the Memorial Fountain presented by Mr. G. W. Childs, of Philadelphia, to Stratford-upon-Avon, passed off under the brightest auspices. Never has the old town celebrated a festive occasion with more enthusiasm or presented itself under better aspects. The weather was perfect. The last after-glow of summer suffused the antique tenements with a softened light, and the streets were radiant with bunting, draping the ancient frontages and suspended in festoons along the eaves. No general holiday had been proclaimed by the authorities, but the townsfolk, of their own prompting, made holiday. The Mayor, Sir Arthur Hodgson, had suggested a partial suspension of business during the ceremonial, but the event quite stirred the pulses of the people and the day became a general Jubilee. Public interest was much more than local. Visitors from London, Birmingham, and other populous centres were attracted and contributed to give Stratford one of the liveliest days in its annals.

"Among the distinguished visitors were United States Minister Phelps, Lord Ronald Gower, Lord De La Warr, Sir Theodore Martin, Sir Philip Cunliffe Owen, Mr. Henry Irving, and the Mayors of Worcester, Lichfield, Coventry, Warwick, and Leamington, who were the guests of the corporation. At noon all these, with many other visitors, had assembled at the Town Hall, whence the Mayor and the members of the corporation, all attired in their official robes, marched in procession to the site of the memorial. Here there had long been assembled a large throng of townsfolk and strangers, who admired the graceful proportions of the fine structure which now associates the name of MR. CHILDS with the history of Stratford-upon-Avon. The crowd was cleared back by a guard of the local volunteer corps, and a square was formed, within which the ceremony was proceeded with. A large marquee had been erected as a precaution against inclement weather, but it was deserted for the space around the fountain."

THE 'HERALD'S' REPORT.

The account of the day and its ceremonies telegraphed to the New York 'Herald' was only less extended than that published by its neighbor the 'World,' but it was still lengthy enough to serve as a brief epitome and chronicle of the notable celebration, its author being Hon. A. Oakey Hall, formerly Mayor of New York City, but at the **time of the** dedication he was, as he now is, an eminent London journalist, representing in the great metropolis with scholarly ability the 'Herald.' Mr. Hall's account is so admirably written, and presents so attractive a view of Stratford on the day of the Fountain's dedi**cation,** as to render its introduction here more than pardonable. Mr. Hall said:—

"The names of WILLIAM SHAKSPEARE and GEORGE WILLIAM CHILDS will be indissolubly united after this day in this city, where the editor's fountain and clock tower were added to the bard's memorials to glorify this historic spot. The Philadelphian's gift was long ago described in the 'Herald' when the designs were adopted. As completed and this morning dedicated, the gift is doubtless one of the most artistic fountains in the world, as will be seen when some of the several thousand photos now multiplying reach New York.

"After several days of wintry weather, this morning came in as a St. Martin's summer day, with bright, warm sunshine. The early trains from London, Leamington, Worcester, Warwick, etc. brought throngs of sightseers. On every side flags abounded, including the Stars and Stripes, fine specimens of which flew from the spire of the Town Hall and the Mayoralty residence, where the Mayor, Sir Arthur Hodgson, entertained Minister Phelps as an especial guest, and Sir Theodore Martin, John Walter, proprietor of the London 'Times,' Sir Philip Cunliffe Owen, Earl De La Warr, Dr. Macaulay, and several other notables from adjacent cities.

"At noon a procession left the Town Hall to march a quarter of a mile to the fountain, which fronts a square formed by the junction of several streets and is looked upon by Shakspeare's house. The procession, headed by the Mayor and Aldermen in full regalia, escorting Mr. Irving and thirty guests, was preceded by a band playing British patriotic airs. On arriving at the variegated granite gift, Mayor Hodgson, in gorgeous robes and chain, presenting a decidedly classic face and figure, took his stand at the foot of the steps leading **up to the** drink-fountain.

"After reading a quaint letter from the **poet** Whittier and another from James Russell Lowell, he briefly explained the object of the gathering, with eulogistic and well-expressed references to MR. CHILDS, and complimentary allusions to America, 'the adopted country of Shakspeare,' and introduced Minister Phelps **as** the representative of the United States. The latter's speech, given with diplomatic **skill,** was short but full of meaning. Everybody awaited Irving, who meantime had taken a position on the second step of the inside structure, partially leaning against the granite wing. At this moment an instantaneous photograph was taken **of** the entire group, to be sent to MR. CHILDS.

"Mr. Irving then, by request, stood within the dry basin in dedicating the gift, and, with fine elocution, made an address lasting a quarter of an hour, in the course of which he said, as a part of the peroration:—

"'**The donor of this** beautiful monument I am happy to claim as a personal friend. MR. GEORGE W. CHILDS **is** not only an admirable representative of the public spirit and enterprising energy of Philadelphia, but he is also a man who has endeared himself to a very wide circle by many generous deeds.

"'I do not wonder at his munificence, for to men like him it is second nature; but I rejoice in the happy inspiration which prompted a gift which so worthily represents the common homage of two great people to the most famous man of **their** common race.

"'The simplest records of Stratford show that this is the Mecca of American pilgrims, and that the place which gave birth to Shakspeare is regarded as the fountain of the mightiest and most enduring inspiration of our mother tongue.'

"The following was his epilogue: 'Let me con-**jure** fancies. Let me picture Shakspeare to-day returning from his bourne to find upon the throne one who rules with gentler sway than the great sovereign that he knew, and yet whose reign has glories more beneficent than those of Elizabeth. We can try to imagine his emotion when he finds this dear England he loved so well expanded beyond seas.

"'We can at least be happy in the thought that when he had mastered the lessons of the conflict which divided us from our kinsmen in America, he would be proud to see in Stratford this gift of a distinguished American citizen—this memorial of our reunion—under the shadow of his undying name.'

"During his speech Mr. Irving referred to the manuscript ode which he had previously read, and which was written for the occasion by Dr. Holmes.

"Then Dr. Macaulay, as a personal friend of MR. CHILDS, and Mr. Irving, representing the authorities, jointly turned on the water into the large drinking-fountain for horses and cattle, the smaller one for dogs and the interior one for thirsty pedestrians, while simultaneously invisible hands inside the clock tower set the hour and started the works. The first flow, however, was caught in a flat glass jar, bought at the bar of the Shakspeare Inn, hard by, and was handed by Sir Philip Cunliffe Owen to Mr. Irving, to be by him presented in person to MR. CHILDS.

"A striking incident here occurred. A large white spitz dog, evidently astray and a stranger to the town, who had gravely joined the procession, next dignifiedly ensconced himself inside the fountain steps and listened in a crouched attitude to the speeches, but when the water was turned on he arose, and approaching Mr. Irving, uttered a slight bark. The tragedian patted the dog amid applause, while J. C. Parkinson and Clement Scott graciously led the animal to a small trough. However, they realized the old maxim about leading a beast to water.

"Next the procession re-formed, the band playing 'Hail Columbia!' and the guests turned their backs on water to take wine and biscuits and face a delightful *menu* at luncheon in the Town Hall banqueting-room, to enter which they filed past a life-size statue of Shakspeare on the porch. Covers had been laid for two hundred under Gainsborough's celebrated picture of Garrick leaning against Shakspeare's bust, Wilkie's picture of Shakspeare, and a full-length portrait of good Queen Anne.

"The *menu* was of aldermanic proportions, consisting of thirty different dishes, with a generous supply of bottles of six species of wine.

"Every dish on the *menu* was illustrated by Shakspearian lines. I give three apt ones: To the galantines of pigeons with mushrooms, this from Henry IV., 'Some pigeons, Davy, and any little kickshaws, tell William the cook.' From the same play to the salads—'Salad was born to do me good.' To tongue this, from 'The Merchant of Venice'— 'Silence is only commendable in a neat's tongue dried.'

"The royal toasts were fully honored. Minister Phelps eulogized President Cleveland and gallantly referred to Mrs. Cleveland. Dr. Macaulay and then Sir Philip Cunliffe Owen responded to the health of MR. CHILDS; but the best speech was by Mr. Irving, responding to the memory of Shakspeare, and concluding thus:—

"'Ladies and gentlemen: In a few days I shall sail for the great country where any worthy representation of Shakspeare on the stage commands as stanch a support from the public as in our own land.

"'I shall carry, as your ambassador to MR. CHILDS, your enthusiastic appreciation of his generous gift.

"'To-day's ceremonial has given infinite pleasure to all, for it has renewed our hallowed associations with the mighty dead and has reminded two great nations of the bond which no calamity can dissolve; and, believe me, it will make every actor in the world-wide sphere of Shakspeare's influence prouder than ever of the calling which I have the privilege of representing here.'

"In response to a call, John Walter, of the London 'Times,' made a few offhand remarks about MR. CHILDS'S hospitality to himself when in America, applying to MR. CHILDS the line about taking the tide at flood which led him on to fortune.

"Next, turning toward Mayor Hodgson, he said, 'We were boys at Eton. Until to-day we have not met in half a century. He was known at school as "Trump Hodgson." When I saw him to-day, my salutation was, "How d'ye do, Trump?" And certainly, along with MR. CHILDS, as I turn from the fountain to the banquet, he has proven himself a very trump.'

"This was heartily received by all the guests, and all separated with the line aptly chosen at the end of the *menu* from 'All's Well That Ends Well:' 'A good traveller is something at the latter end of a dinner.'"

A CONSENSUS OF PRAISE.

With no known exception the leading newspapers of the United States printed special or Associated Press despatches from Stratford, which were generally accompanied by editorial remarks referring to the celebration of the previous day. Of the several hundred appreciative editorial articles which were kindly sent me by their writers I have thought it not unfit to use a few to round out this history of the Shakspeare Memorial on the Avonside. That which so attractively characterized all the elaborate reports and remarks of both the English and American journals was the common recognition and fine appreciation of the spirit of international good-will which inspired MR. CHILDS to set up there, near by the poet's home, an enduring memorial of the love and reverence of all English-speaking people for that sublime genius who filled not only the spacious times of Great Elizabeth, but all times since with the wondrous wisdom and beauty of his thought and feeling.

AT MR. CHILDS'S HOME.

The newspapers of Philadelphia, on the day following the celebration at Shakspeare's birthplace, published lengthy accounts by their special foreign correspondents of the ceremonies, which were supplemented by editorial comments. The spirit of them all was sufficiently suggested by the following editorial remarks of the 'Evening Telegraph':—

"The dedication yesterday—the full particulars of which were published in our issue of yesterday afternoon—of the beautiful Memorial Fountain presented to the town of Stratford-upon-Avon, the birthplace of Shakspeare, by MR. GEORGE W. CHILDS, was a very interesting and imposing demonstration. Mr. Irving, as the representative of the scholarly and artistic traditions of the English theatre, was very appropriately the orator of the occasion; while the graceful letter from Mr. James Russell Lowell, the poem by Dr. Oliver Wendell Holmes, and the address of Minister Phelps, testified to the American interest in the occasion, and to our claims to be inheritors with the English of the glorious works which the genius of Shakspeare produced. Abundant praise was bestowed **by all the participants on MR. CHILDS for his enlightened liberality, and it was agreed upon all sides that the Fountain was a very beautiful work, and the fact that it was** the gift of an American gave it a particular value. Mr. Lowell, in his letter, made a graceful and appropriate allusion to the fact that as it was Washington Irving who first embodied in proper language the emotion which Stratford-upon-Avon awakens in the mind of the pilgrim, so it was a countryman of Irving who had, in 'a solid and durable way,' said one of those agreeable things which seem to make Englishmen and Americans regard themselves as having a com**mon** interest in many matters besides the fame and works of Shakspeare."

In its issue of October 18th, the 'Times' of Philadelphia added this just and appropriate comment to the general expression, in similar vein, of the English and American press:—

"In erecting monuments to other people in various parts of the world, MR. CHILDS is perpetuating the memory of his own public-spirited generosity. It might be said that Shakspeare needed no monumental shaft, and least of all in Stratford-upon-Avon, where everything speaks the poet's name. But the structure which was dedicated yesterday is the first distinct recognition at modern hands of that which has made the old town forever famous, and there is an especial significance in the manner of its erection, which makes it the New World's tribute to the genius whose sway is acknowledged far beyond even Victoria's wide realm, and has equally enriched all English-speaking people under every flag. The monument is thus far more than an individual gift to the town of Stratford. It has its international significance as well, and is a token of the universality of those higher interests of our race that transcend all mere political boundaries."

FRIENDS ELSEWHERE.

The editorial references of the American newspaper press were peculiarly appreciative, the New York 'Times' of October 18th saying:—

"The proceedings at Stratford-upon-Avon on Monday in dedicating to the memory of Shakspeare the Memorial Fountain presented to the town by Mr. GEORGE W. CHILDS, of Philadelphia, afforded one of those occasions upon which Englishmen and Americans, especially the latter, delight to recognize the common ties of tradition and literature which unite the two peoples in a relationship made too strong by natural kinship to be severed by oft-recurring conflicts of interest. It is doubtful if, even in England, there is such a universal reading and understanding of the works of Shakspeare among the mass of the people as in this country, or such a general appreciation of the grand heritage of English literature. The sympathy produced by this common possession of a language and literature is stronger than is generally acknowledged, and it is the basis of a mutual understanding that ought to be a guarantee of perpetual friendly relations. Incidents like that of yesterday, brought about by a generous and public-spirited American, are of value in reminding the two nations of what they have in common, and in teaching them to be tolerant in those things in which they differ."

The 'Times's' neighbor, the 'Commercial Advertiser,' made the following editorial comment on the celebration :—

"The exercises which marked the dedication of the Childs Memorial Fountain to Shakspeare at Stratford-upon-Avon drew together yesterday a notable company, in which America was well represented. The gift itself came from this country, and the principal and characteristic parts of the services were American also. The letter from Mr. Lowell, the poem by Dr. Holmes, and the active participation in the exercises by Minister Phelps gave a tone to the occasion which stamped it as distinctively American. And it may be added that the memorial theatre and museum that is erected hard by the site of the fountain owes much to the interest felt in Shakspeare's fame by citizens of the United States.

"Our love and reverence for the Stratford poet are natural and easy of explanation. As Mr. Irving said, Shakspeare's tomb is a literary Mecca for all English-speaking peoples, and especially for that branch of the family that quit the fatherland not far from the poet's time and carried with them the English he and his neighbors spoke. The claim is sometimes made, and perhaps should be made with greater seriousness than we are inclined to use, that Americans speak better English than the present inhabitants of England. We shall not now defend either side of such a contention, but it is worth while to notice that such a close Shakspearian student as Mr. Irving—who can speak, too, from extensive observation and a large acquaintance in America—finds occasion to say that 'some of the idioms which are supposed to be of American invention can be traced back to Shakspeare,' and that it is more than probable that among the original settlers of this country were **men** who had sat in the Globe Theatre and brought away from it 'something of Shakspeare's imagery and vivid portraiture.'

"It is fitting, therefore, that Americans should take a conspicuous share in any memorials which gratitude may raise to the greatest master of our language. His reign, as Mr. Lowell happily expressed it, is not subject to political vicissitudes. He holds his possessions, on either shore of the dividing sea, 'in memory and imagination by a title such as no conquest ever established, and no revolution can ever overthrow.' That, in these latter days, presumptuous rebels have contested his claims to the world's affectionate homage did not disturb yesterday's devotions at his tomb, and will not, we fancy, ever shake, to any noticeable degree, the allegiance of mankind."

FROM THE FAR WEST.

Under the caption of "A New Fraternity," the 'Evening Wisconsin,' of Milwaukee, thus happily expressed the full and perfect meaning of MR. CHILDS's gift as well as the common sentiment of the broad western world for which it has authority to speak:—

"More than skilful diplomacy could do in a score of years in cementing friendship and unifying sentiment between England and America, was accomplished at Stratford-upon-Avon yesterday by the wise generosity of one man, and he an American citizen.

"With imposing ceremony, far more heartfelt and cordial than is often witnessed on any public occasion, there was presented to the village of Stratford the superb and symbolical Memorial Fountain to Shakspeare, the erection of which had been ordered by GEORGE W. CHILDS, of Philadelphia, with the injunction, 'Spare no expense.' 'I wish,' said MR. CHILDS, in one of his letters to the Mayor of Stratford, 'to present a gift to Shakspeare's town worthy of his great name.'

"In his Memorial, thus modestly given, MR. CHILDS has rendered a better service to America than to England, or even to Shakspeare's village of Stratford. He has indicated and expressed in the best manner the American appreciation of the immortal work Shakspeare did, and the American reverence of what, in his peerless genius, Shakspeare was. He has crystallized into something tangible, which all the world will permanently look upon, the intangible fact that America, the babe among nations in age and in the development of her literature, is not a babe, but an equal of every nation, in her intelligent, discriminating understanding of Shakspeare as 'the fountain of the mightiest and most enduring inspiration of the English tongue.'

"And as a tribute to England almost as much as in its symbolical aspect, the gift is of rare and lasting worth. It is a monument set up to be read by Americans and Englishmen of all time as the sign of kinship in nationality—marking us one in language and sympathies, and, to an extent, one in aims and methods for the on-pushing of the world's civilization. It was a graceful act to set an American memorial on English soil in honor of an Englishman; and it will stand as one more welcome obstacle in the way of estrangements between the two peoples.

"The ceremonial of yesterday's dedication was in every detail faultless. The weather was perfect; the concourse of people vast and their deportment cordial; the gathering of distinguished Englishmen and Americans was large and representative, and the addresses and letters were of signal merit and appropriateness. The letter from James Russell Lowell, the genial, able speech by Henry Irving, and the poem contributed by our revered Oliver Wendell Holmes, were in their matter and manner and rendition beyond criticism.

"It was a good day and a good happening for Englishmen and Americans. The keynote in all that was said and done was 'fraternity.' The modest Philadelphia philanthropist, in pleasing a noble impulse born primarily out of his regard for genius, has rendered a permanent service to patriotism and to the brotherhood of nations."

THE VOICE OF THE SOUTH.

The Daily 'News,' of Baltimore, referring to the universal interest which everything of moment relating to Shakspeare creates, said:—

"The description of the dedication of MR. CHILDS's Fountain has been given as much space by the press—British and American—as some great political event might have been. And yet it was an occurrence of little international significance—merely a tribute paid by a private American citizen to the greatest genius of England. But this affection and admiration for Shakspeare are so profound and universal—so much like a religion—that every fact relating to him or his memory excites almost world-wide attention. More closely and zealously every year is he studied, and more earnestly and pertinaciously is the attempt made to penetrate the beautiful mystery of his genius. Never were there so many books published about him as now, although those already concerned with the subject make a vast and wonderful library. Who has computed the number and variety of the editions of his plays? **And** yet new ones are constantly coming forth. In every direction the antiquarians are delving for some new facts which might throw a light, if only a single gleam, upon the history of this bewildering genius. At the smallest discovery, or even shred of evidence that leads to an inference, the world pauses in its work and listens all agog.

"The Stratford ceremonies were in every way interesting. MR. CHILDS, in presenting the beautiful fountain **to the town,** only did what many others would like to have done. Some other object **he** might have offered—there are many ways in which his admiration for the poet might have expressed itself; but, after all, **as** Mr. Irving remarked, there seems something particularly appropriate in the fountain which has been erected in the middle of the quaint old town, for the use of all, and for beast as well as man.

"The occasion was altogether one of which Americans may be as proud as MR. CHILDS must be. As Irving remarked, it is the Americans who have always been foremost in making pilgrimages and paying tributes to the Stratford poet. MR. CHILDS has done many things to show the exalted character of his mind and his goodness of heart, and it seems that he could not rest until he **had** made a gift **of** this beautiful fountain—according to all accounts, one of the most artistic in the world—to the memory of Shakspeare. The day was a lovely one, and everything connected with the ceremonies passed off in the most complete and satisfactory manner."

WILLIAM WINTER, POET AND DRAMATIC CRITIC, TELLS THE STORY OF THE FOUNTAIN.

No one, however, has more pleasantly told the story of the Fountain than has Mr. William Winter, the poet, journalist, and critic. His sympathy with the purpose of the giver of the Memorial is as broad as his reverent love for Shakspeare is profound, and to both which sympathy and love he has borne testimony in books, essays, poems, letters, and criticisms. He is one of the most brilliant of American writers, and one whose audience, while always large, is always fit. 'Harper's Weekly' of October 22, 1887, published an excellent illustration of the Stratford Fountain, accompanied by a characteristic sketch by Mr. Winter which cannot without impairing its fair symmetry be curtailed. Mr. Winter said:—

"American interest in Stratford-upon-Avon springs out of a love for the works of Shakspeare as profound and passionate as that of the most sensitive and reverent of the poet's own countrymen. It was the father of American literature—Washington Irving—who in modern times made the first pilgrimage to that Holy Land, and set the good example, which since has been followed by thousands, of worship at the shrine of Shakspeare. It was an American—the alert and expeditious Mr. Barnum—who, by suddenly proposing to buy the Shakspeare cottage and transfer it to America, frightened the English into buying it as a treasure for the nation. It is in part to Americans that Stratford owes the picturesque and useful Shakspeare Memorial; for, while the land on which it stands was given by that liberal and public-spirited citizen of Stratford, Mr. Charles Edward Flower—a kindly gentleman and a sound and fine Shakspeare scholar, as his acting edition of eighteen of the plays may testify—and while money to pay for the building of it was freely contributed by rich residents of Warwickshire and by men of all ranks throughout the kingdom, the gifts and labors of Americans were not lacking to that good cause. Edwin Booth was one of the earliest contributors to the Memorial Fund. The names of Mr. Herman Vezin, Mr. M. D. Conway, Mr. W. H. Reynolds, Mrs. Bateman, and Mrs. Louise Chandler Moulton appear in the first list of its subscribers. Miss Kate Field worked for its advancement with remarkable energy and practical success. Miss Mary Anderson acted for its benefit, on August 29, 1885, giving in its own theatre the first performance of Rosalind that she ever gave, and, like Edwin Booth, she is now one of the Governors of the Shakspeare Memorial Association. In the Church of the Holy Trinity, on the brink of the lovely Avon, where Shakspeare's dust is buried, a beautiful stained window, illustrative, by Scriptural symbols, of that solemn epitome of human life which the poet gives in the speech of Jaques on the seven ages of man, evinces the practical devotion of the American pilgrim; and this assuredly thrills his heart with reverent joy when he sees the soft light, streaming through its pictured panes, fall gently on the poet's grave.

"Wherever in Stratford you come upon anything that was ever associated, even remotely, with the name and fame of Shakspeare, there you will surely find the gracious tokens of American homage. The libraries of the birthplace and **of** the Memorial contain gifts of American books. New Place and Anne Hathaway's Cottage are never omitted from the American traveller's round of visitations and duty of practical tribute. The Falcon, with its store of relics, including the oak wainscot, that were in the parlor of the place when Shakspeare owned it; the romantic Shakspeare Inn, with its rambling passages, its quaint rooms named after Shakspeare's characters, its antique bar parlor, and Mrs. Justin's fine collection of autographs and pictures; the Grammar School, in which it is likely that the poet, 'with shining morning face' of boyhood, was once a pupil; the Town Hall, adorned with Gainsborough's eloquent portrait of Garrick to which no engraving does justice; the Guild Chapel; the Clopton Bridge; the Old Mill; the foot-path across fields and roads to Shottery, bosomed in great elms; and the ancient house of many gables, four miles away, at Wilmcote, which was the home of Mary Arden, Shakspeare's mother—each of these storied places receives in turn the tribute of the wandering American, and each repays him a hundredfold in charming suggestiveness of association, in high thought, and in the lasting impulse of sweet and soothing poetic reverie. At the Red Horse Inn, where Mr. Colbourne maintains all the traditions of old-fashioned English hospitality, he finds his home, well pleased to sit and dream in Washington Irving's parlor, while the night deepens and the clock in the distant tower murmurs drowsily in its sleep. Those who will may mock at his enthusiasm. He would not feel it but for the spell that Shakspeare's genius has cast upon the world. He ought to be glad and grateful that he can feel that spell; and since he does feel it nothing could be more natural than his desire to signify that he too, though born far away from the old home of his race and separated from it by three thousand miles of stormy ocean, has still his part in the divine legacy of Shakspeare, the treasure and the glory of the English tongue.

"A noble token of this American sentiment and a permanent object of patriotic interest to the pilgrim in Stratford is supplied by the Jubilee gift of a Drinking Fountain, made to that city by GEORGE W. CHILDS, of Philadelphia. It never is a surprise to hear of some new instance of that good man's constant activity and splendid generosity in good works: it is only an accustomed pleasure. With fine-art testimonials in the Old World as well as at home his name will always be honorably associated. A few years ago he presented a superb Window of stained glass to Westminster Abbey, to commemorate in the Poet's Corner George Herbert and William Cowper. He has since given to St. Margaret's Church, Westminster, where Skelton and Sir James Harrington (1611–1677) were entombed, and where was buried the headless body of Sir Walter Raleigh, a pictorial Window commemorative of John Milton. His Fountain at Stratford was dedicated on October 17th, 1887, with appropriate ceremonies conducted by **the** city's Mayor, Sir Arthur Hodgson, of Clopton Hall, and **amid** general rejoicing. The countrymen of MR. CHILDS are not **less** interested in this structure than the commu**nity that** it was intended to honor and benefit. They observe with satisfaction and pride that he has made this beneficent, beautiful, and opulent offering to a town which for all of them is hallowed by exalted associations, and for many of them is endeared by delightful memories. They sympathize also with the motive **and feeling** that prompted him **to** offer his gift as one among many memorials of the fiftieth year of the reign of Queen Victoria. **It is not** every man who knows how to give with grace, and the good deed **is** 'done double' that is done at the right time. Stratford had long been in need of such a fountain **as MR.** CHILDS has given, and therefore it satisfies a public want, at the same time that it serves a purpose of ornamentation and bespeaks and strengthens a bond of international sympathy. Rother Square, in which the structure stands, is the most considerable open tract in Stratford, and is situated near to the centre of the town, on the west side. There, as also at the intersection of High and Bridge streets, which are the principal thoroughfares of the city, the farmers, at stated intervals, range their beasts and wagons and hold a market. It is easy to foresee that Rother Square, as now embellished with this superb monument, which combines a convenient clock-tower, a place of rest and refreshment for man, commodious drinking troughs for horses, cattle, dogs, and sheep, will become the agricultural centre of the region.

"The base of the monument is made of Peterhead granite; the superstructure is of **gray stone** —from Bolton, Yorkshire. The height **of the tower** is sixty feet. On the north side a stream of water flowing from a bronze spout falls into a polished granite basin. On the south side a door opens into the interior. The decorations include sculptures of the arms of Great Britain alternated with the eagle and stripes of the American Republic. In the second story of the tower, lighted by glazed arches, is placed an illuminated clock, and on the outward faces of the third story appear four dials. **There** are four turrets surrounding a central spire, each surmounted with a gilded vane. The inscriptions at the base are these:

I.

'The gift of an American citizen, GEORGE W. CHILDS, of
Philadelphia, to the town of Shakspeare, in the
Jubilee Year of Queen Victoria.'

II.

'In her days every man shall eat, in safety
Under his own vine, what he plants; and sing
The merry songs of peace to all his neighbors.
God shall be truly known: and those about her
From her shall read the perfect ways of honor,
And by those claim their greatness, not by blood.
              Henry VIII., Act V., Scene IV.'

III.

'Honest water, which ne'er left man i' the mire.
      Timon of Athens, Act I., Scene II.'

IV.

'Ten thousand honors and blessings on the bard who
has gilded the dull realities of life with innocent illusions.—*Washington Irving's Stratford-upon-Avon*.'

"Stratford-upon-Avon, fortunate in many things, is especially fortunate in being situated at a considerable distance **from the main line of any railway.** Two railroads indeed skirt the town, but both are branches, and travel upon them has not yet become too frequent. Stratford, therefore, still retains a measure of its ancient isolation and consequently of its quaintness. Antique customs are still prevalent there and odd characters may still be encountered. The current of village gossip flows with incessant vigor, and nothing happens in the place that is not thoroughly discussed. An event so important as the establishment of this American Fountain has of course excited great interest throughout Warwickshire. It would be pleasant to hear the talk of those old cronies who drift into the bar-parlor of the Red Horse Hotel, on a Saturday evening—the learned Guppy, resting from the labors of Her Majesty's Post-office; the genial Cole, fresh from his auctioneer's pulpit; the aristocratic Vet, whose visage so plainly manifests his noble origin; and Richard Savage, scholar and antiquary—as they comment on the liberal American whose generosity has thus enriched and beautified their town. This Red Horse circle is but one of many in which the name of GEORGE W. CHILDS is spoken with esteem and cherished with affection. The present writer has made many visits to Stratford and has passed much time there, and he has observed on many occasions the admiration and gratitude of the Warwickshire people for the American philanthropist. In the library of

Charles Edward Flower at Avonbank, in the gardens of Edgar Flower on the Hill, in the lovely home of Alderman Bird, at the table of Sir Arthur Hodgson in Clopton Hall, and in many other representative places, he has heard that name spoken, and always with delight and honor. Time will only deepen and widen the loving respect with which it is hallowed. In England, more than anywhere else on earth, the record of good deeds is made permanent, not alone with imperishable symbols, but in the hearts of the people. The inhabitants of Warwickshire, guarding and maintaining their Stratford Fountain, will never forget by whom it was given. Wherever you go in the British islands you find memorials of the Poet and of individuals who have done good in their time, and you find that these memorials are respected and preserved. Warwickshire abounds with them. One of the most conspicuous objects in the landscape as you draw near to Stratford is the monolith on Welcombe Hill that commemorates the virtues and public services of Mark Phillips—long a member of Parliament for Manchester—and the abiding fraternal love that caused it to be placed. Welcombe Manor-house stands on the site of the hall that was the residence of Shakspeare's friend, John-a-Combe. **On the road from** Stratford to

Warwick the traveller passes near to one of the loveliest churches in all that region, a costly edifice commemorative of the late Miss Rylander, whose whole life was passed in doing good. At Leamington they have even erected a monument, in a public square containing many superb trees, to honor the worthy citizen and his wife by whose munificence those trees were preserved. Many such memorials might be indicated. Each one of them takes its place in the regard, and gradually becomes entwined with the experience, of the whole community. **So it will be with the** CHILDS FOUNTAIN **at Stratford.** The children trooping home from school will drink of it and sport in its shadow, and reading upon **its base** the name of its founder will think with pleasure of a good man's gift. It lies directly in the track of travel between Banbury and Birmingham, and many weary men and horses will pause beside it every day for a moment of rest and refreshment. On festival days it will be hung with garlands, while all around it the air is glad with music. And often in the long, sweet gloaming of the summer times to come the rower on the limpid river Avon that murmurs by the ancient town of Shakspeare will pause with suspended oar to hear its silver chimes. If the founder of this

Fountain had been capable of a selfish thought, he could have taken no way better or more certain than this for the perpetuation of his own name in the affectionate esteem of one of the loveliest places and one of the most refined communities in the world.

"The autumn in England is well advanced, and all the country ways of **lovely** Warwickshire are strewn with fallen leaves. But the cool winds of October are sweet and bracing, the dark waters of the Avon, shimmering in mellow sunlight and frequent shadow, flow gently past the hallowed church, and the reaped and gleaned and empty meadows invite to many a healthful ramble far and wide over the country of Shakspeare. It is a good time to be there. Now will the robust pedestrian make his jaunt to Charlecote Park and Hampton Lucy, to Stoneleigh Abbey, to Warwick and Kenilworth, to Guy's Cliff, with its weird avenue of semi-blasted trees, to the Blacklow Hill, where sometimes at still midnight the shuddering peasant hears the ghostly funeral bell of Sir Piers Gaveston sounding ruefully from out the black and gloomy woods, and to many another historic haunt and high poetic shrine. All the country-side is full of storied resorts and **cozy** nooks and comfortable inns. But neither now nor hereafter will it be otherwise than grateful and touching to such an explorer of haunted Warwickshire to see, among the emblems of poetry and romance which are its chief glory, this new token of American sentiment and friendship, the Drinking Fountain of Stratford, the gift of GEORGE W. CHILDS.

"WILLIAM WINTER."

I know of no words which have been spoken to show the reason for the good-will that should forever be maintained by the people of England and America, each for the other, which more clearly exhibit it, than those of "Honest John Bright," who, in the dark days of the Republic's struggle for life, speaking in 1864 to a great multitude of his countrymen in the city of London, asked them: "Can we forget that, after all, we are one nation, having two governments; that we are the same noble and heroic race; that half the English family is on this side of the Atlantic, in its ancient home, and the other half—there being no room for them here—is settled on the American continent?"

The spirit of the question asked by the Great Commoner, and which inspired him to sympathize with this government of the people, for the people, and by the people, is the very sentient one which inspired MR. CHILDS to erect on Avon's bank the Fountain to Shakspeare—and to set up elsewhere in England's sacred shrines other fit memorials to venerable British worthies—the story of which is herein told.

THE HERBERT AND COWPER MEMORIAL

IN

WESTMINSTER ABBEY.

THE HERBERT AND COWPER MEMORIAL IN WESTMINSTER ABBEY.

THAT which came next in his love for his holy office to ARTHUR PENRHYN STANLEY, D.D., Dean of Westminster, was the Abbey, the story of which he has so fully and pleasantly told in his "Historical Memorials." The first chapter of this scholarly work, which he wrought out to so noble a conclusion, has the following introduction, copied from a contemporaneous biography of Edward the Confessor in a Harleian manuscript: "THE FOUNDATION OF WESTMINSTER ABBEY. The devout King destined to God that place, both for that it was near unto the famous and wealthy City of London, and also had a pleasant situation amongst fruitful fields lying round about it, with the principal river running hard by, bringing it from all parts of the world great variety of wares and merchandise of all sorts to the city adjoining; but chiefly for the love of the CHIEF APOSTLE, whom he reverenced with a special and singular affection."

Dean Stanley never spoke of the Abbey save with the tenderest, most reverential feeling. He knew all that could be known about it—its foundation, its growth, its legendary and historical origin; its relics, its tombs, its shrines, its chapels, its transepts, its cloisters, and its illustrious dead. For years he had moved and had his being among them. Through them he lived in all times of England's triumphs and defeats. To his broad and all-embracing mind there was no difference between the ashes lying there of the courtly nobles of Charles I. and those of the rude Titans of the Commonwealth. It was this feeling which enabled him to say, in Chapter IV. of his "Memorials":—

"Of all the characteristics of Westminster Abbey that which most endears it to the nation and gives most force to its name—which has, more than anything else, made it the home of the people of England and the most venerated fabric of the English Church—is not so much its glory as the seat of the coronations or as the sepulchre of the kings; not so much its school, or its monastery, or its chapter, or its sanctuary, as the fact that it is the resting-place of famous Englishmen, from every rank and creed and every form of mind and genius. It is not only Rheims Cathedral and St. Denys both in one, but it is also what the Pantheon was intended to be to France—what the Valhalla is to Germany—what Santa Croce is to Italy. It is this aspect which, more than any other, won for it the delightful visits of Addison in the 'Spectator,' of Steele in the 'Tatler,' of Goldsmith in 'The Citizen of the World,' of Charles Lamb in 'Elia,' of Washington Irving in 'The Sketch Book.' It is this which inspired the saying of Nelson, 'A Peerage — or Westminster Abbey!' and which has intertwined it with so many eloquent passages of Macaulay. It is this which gives point to the allusions of recent statesmen least inclined to draw illustrations from ecclesiastical buildings. It is this which gives most promise of vitality to the whole institution. Kings are no longer buried within its walls; even the splendor of pageants has ceased to attract; but the desire to be interred in Westminster Abbey is still as strong as ever."

Nowhere in his story of the famous Abbey does the erudite Dean exhibit so much feeling in the telling of it as in that part which has to do with the great dead poets of England. The historian lingers long and fondly in the 'Poet's Corner,' for, though they all lie not there, monuments are therein erected to the memory of Chaucer, Spenser, Shakspeare, Drayton, Ben Jonson, Ayton, Davenant, Cowley, Dryden, Milton, Butler, Rowe, **Steele, Addison**, Congreve, Prior, Gay, Pope, Thomson, and Gray.

Dean Stanley's cultivated and refined mind sympathized profoundly with the men of genius who, through recurring ages, have by their so potent art made glorious the Literature of England, and probably with **no** others more than with these two, among the greatest and sweetest singers of them all—the Christian Poets, Herbert and Cowper—to whose genius there had been no memorials set up in the Abbey, though it was long his most ardent wish there should be. Among those to whom Dean Stanley communicated his desire **was his friend,** MR. GEORGE W. CHILDS, of Philadelphia, and **with** what sequence is thus briefly told by the Rev. **Alex**ander B. Grosart, in a note to his complete works of George Herbert, printed for private circulation only: "To the praise **of** GEORGE W. CHILDS, Esq., of Philadelphia, U. S. A., **be it** recorded that, on learning the wish of the **Dean of** Westminster and others to place **a** Memorial Window **in** our great

Abbey, in honor of George Herbert and **William Cowper**, as Westminster school boys, he spontaneously and large-heartedly expressed his readiness to furnish such a Window at his own cost. The generous offer was cordially accepted."

MR. CHILDS was almost as well known in England as in America. His "House Beautiful" in Philadelphia had long been famed as the home of the most splendid and refined hospitality which had been gratefully enjoyed by many of the most distinguished Englishmen visiting America. Among them was the Very Rev., learned, and good Dr. Stanley, Dean of Westminster. In a sermon preached in St. James's P. E. Church, Philadelphia, on the morning of September 29, 1878, the Dean, then the guest of MR. CHILDS, said:—

"It has been one happy characteristic of the Church of England that it has retained both sides of the Christian character within its pale. There is in Westminster Abbey a Window dear to American hearts, because erected by an honored citizen of Philadelphia, in which these two elements are presented side by side. On the one hand, the sacred poet most cherished by the ecclesiastical, royalist, priest-like phase of the Church, George Herbert; on the other hand, the sacred poet most cherished by the Puritan, austere, lay phase of the Church, William Cowper. That diversity is an example of the way in which God's will is wrought on earth as it is in heaven. I have said that we do not speculate on the names or natures of angels, yet as symbols and outlines of the divine operations they may be most useful to us. In the rabbinical and mediæval theology this diversity used to be represented by the manifold titles of the various principalities and powers. Most of these have now dropped out of use; but there are some few which, either from their mention in the biblical or the apocryphal books, or from the transfiguring hand of artistic or poetic genius, have survived."

The Window dedicated to Herbert and Cowper, which has become one of the conspicuous Memorials of Westminster Abbey, owes its place there to the strong and abiding love which this great English divine had for this country, and to Mr. CHILDS's recognition of the fraternity of feeling which nature has planted deep in the hearts of Englishmen and Americans.

In concluding a most appreciative and graceful tribute to the character of Dean Stanley, then lately gone to his reward, the PUBLIC LEDGER, on the 20th of July, 1881, said: "He believed in a National Church, but his Anglicanism reached **across the water, and** he was fonder and more appreciative of this country than many a citizen of the United States. **Freedom** and reverence, peace born of struggle, and faith in justice worth hard knocks, the charity that comes of knowledge, not of indifference, **a** prayer 'that we may not be persecutors,' a creed like the rainbow, **that** spanned from the horizon to the zenith—these were **the** rich gifts of Stanley's mind, and his legacy to the world are his twin beliefs in unswerving law and all-surrounding love." It was out of his love for the people of the United States—and **of his** perception of the common bonds that bound and made them one with Englishmen—that the Herbert and Cowper Memorial grew. There was, at the time the request for the Window was made and freely responded to, the same thought in the minds of both Dean Stanley and MR. GEORGE W. CHILDS— the thought that, if there were set up in the venerable Abbey, the last resting-place of so many eminent Englishmen, a Memorial to those great worthies, Herbert and Cowper, by an American citizen, who was indisputably a representative of American thought and feeling, it would be, so long as time spared that ancient edifice, a token of the cordial sympathy existing between the two countries.

THE SHARE OF AMERICA IN WESTMINSTER ABBEY.

When in 1867 Sir Charles Wentworth Dilke had finished the story of his travels through the British Colonies and the United States, he could find no title so fit for his attractive work as that of "Greater Britain." He saw, during his protracted visit to this country, only his own country magnified in area, population, wealth, and greatness. He found here the same manners and customs as those of his own land; here he also found the same language, the same political institutions, the same literature, the same art, the same science, the same religion. He was quick to perceive that they of Old England and of New England, of Great Britain and the United States, were one people in their love of virtue, freedom, intelligence, courage, and in their vast, far-reaching enterprise. The broad ocean separated them; prejudices, growing out of misunderstandings, had sometimes caused them often to look askance at each other, to regard each other with distrust. But, despite all prejudices and misunderstandings, they were and are as one in **all** that proclaims the identity of the same people, though living apart.

This thought or sentiment, it need not be said, is not a new one, but as old, at least, in the minds of Englishmen and Americans as was the Mayflower on the day there passed over **her** side to Plymouth Rock the Pilgrim **Fathers.** But again, and a thousand times again, **has it been** newly formulated, and most eloquently, by that learned and devout scholar, F. W. Farrar, D. D., Archdeacon of West-**minster,** in a paper of great international interest and attractiveness contributed by him to 'Harper's Magazine' of January, 1888, which bears the title of "The Share of America in Westminster Abbey."

The Venerable Archdeacon, **whose** fame for piety and learning is as great in this country as in his own, begins his brilliant paper with the words following:—

"Westminster Abbey is most frequently entered by the great northern door, usually known as Solomon's Porch, now in course of a splendid restoration, which will soon be completed. I will, however, ask the courteous American visitor to walk through St. Margaret's Church-yard, and round the western façade of the Abbey, and to enter by the door under Sir Christopher Wren's towers, opposite the memorial raised by Westminster scholars to their school-fellows who died in the Crimean war. **Pass through the western door, and pause for a moment**

> ' **Where** bubbles burst, and folly's dancing foam
> Melts if it cross the threshold.'

Of all the glory of this symbolic architecture, of the awe-inspiring grandeur and beauty of **this** great Minster, which makes us feel at once that

> ' They dreamt not of a perishable home
> Who thus could build,'

how much may be claimed in part by America?

"In one sense *all* of it which belongs to the epoch which elapsed between the age of Edward the Confessor and the disastrous days of Charles **I. and** Archbishop Laud. An English writer who lives in America has said that '**in** signing away his own empire George III. did not sign away the empire of English liberty, of English law, of English literature, of English blood, of English religion, or of the English tongue.' Americans enjoy, no less than we, the benefit of the Great Charter, the Petition of Right, the Habeas Corpus Act. They need not go back for their history to Indian annals or Icelandic sagas. Theirs are the palaces of the Plantagenets, the cathedrals which enshrine our old religion, the illustrious Hall **in** which the long line of our great judges reared by their decisions the fabric of our law, the gray colleges in which our intellect and science found their earliest home, the graves where our heroes and sages and poets sleep. Indeed, I have understated their share in the Abbey. It reaches down, not only to the days of the Pilgrim Fathers, but to the War of Independence. Chatham and Burke and Barré as well as Patrick Henry advocated the American cause, which engaged the sympathy of the great mass of Englishmen, if not that of Grenville and North."

The recognition both by Dean Stanley and by Mr. Childs of the truth of that which Archdeacon Farrar so eloquently said had been previously demonstrated by the setting up in the ancient Abbey of the Memorial to Herbert and Cowper of which, in the above-quoted paper, Archdeacon Farrar says, after referring to the monuments to Kingsley and Craggs: "There are two other memorials which combine with these to give to this spot in the Abbey the name of the 'Little Poets' Corner.' They are the stained glass Windows in memory of George Herbert and William Cowper. They belong entirely to America, for they are the gift of an American citizen, my honored friend, Mr. George William Childs, of Philadelphia. In the stained glass are the effigies of the **two** poets. Both of them were Westminster boys, and the most beautiful representatives of all that **is** holy in two very opposite schools of religious thought. It was a happy inspiration which suggested the erection of this Window. George Herbert and William Cowper were well deserving of Memorials in the Abbey, apart from the fact that they had so often played in its cloisters and worshiped in its choir. The combination of the two suggests the higher unity which reconciles all minor points of ecclesiastical **difference.**"

HERBERT.

Gentle Izaak Walton concluded the remarkable sketch of the life of the pious scholar and poet, George Herbert, which is one of the noblest ornaments of our literature, in these words: "Thus he lived, and thus he died like a saint, unspotted of the world, full of alms-deeds, full of humility, and all the examples of a virtuous life; which I cannot conclude better than with this borrowed observation:—

"'All must to their cold graves;
But the religious actions of the just
Smell sweet in death, and blossom in the dust.'

"Mr. George Herbert's have done so to this, and will doubtless do so to succeeding generations. I have but this to say more of him, that if Andrew Melville died before him, then George Herbert died without an enemy. I wish (if God be so pleased) that I may be so happy as to die like him."

In the estimation of those of wisest censure there are none of the old English Divines or sacred poets whose fame is more deserved, or who are more reverenced by those who speak the language in which the "holy Herbert" gave his writings, in prose and verse, to the world.

COWPER.

On the long roll of England's distinguished men of letters there are few names which shine with so strong, steady, and enduring a light as that of William Cowper. There has been no lessening of his great fame with the passing of time; it was long ago conceded that by his poems he had not only raised "to himself an imperishable name," but that he had added enduring beauty to the English language. His is a name which is not only reverently cherished in the affections, but which appeals to the best thought, high conscience, and lofty sentiment of all men of noble mind.

When MR. CHILDS undertook the fulfilment of the desire of his friend, the Very Rev. Dean of Westminster, to set up the Memorial Window in the Abbey to Herbert and Cowper, the same thought inspired them both—the thought that if the object were accomplished by an American it would be accepted by every Englishman as a tribute of brothers to brothers. The works of these sacred singers live after them in the love and admiration of all English-speaking peoples, and nowhere more truly than among the people of this broad land. The Window of Westminster, though the munificent gift of but one of them, represents the common reverence for the great poet of all Americans of gentle, pious feeling, as his songs were sung for those of all lands of refined natures and devout aspirations.

STANLEY.

DEAN STANLEY'S STORY OF THE WINDOWS.

In 'Sunday at Home,' a magazine of high character, published in London (in the number for June,

1877), there appeared, as a frontispiece, a colored illustration of the Herbert and Cowper Memorial Window, with reference to which Dean **Stanley** contributed the following explanatory note:—

"The southwest corner of the Abbey—once the Abbot's private chapel, then the Baptistery, and now **the** Lay Clerks' vestry—was selected some twenty years ago as the place for the erection of the statue of **the** poet Wordsworth, probably in connection with **the font.** Within the last ten years the present Dean resolved to make it a Second Poet's Corner—chiefly for sacred poets—in order to relieve the great pressure on the South transept. Accordingly, when a **munificent** admirer of Keble—the late Hon. Edward Twistleton—wished to place a bust of the poet in **the** Abbey, the arch next to Wordsworth was chosen for **it.** Since that time Maurice, the theologian, and Kingsley, theologian, novelist, but chiefly poet, have followed. Their busts are on each side of Craggs, the friend of Pope and Addison.

"When MR. GEORGE W. CHILDS, of Philadelphia, with truly American generosity, most generously complied with **my** request that he should give a **Window of stained** glass, **it was** suggested to **him that it should** be placed **in this** chapel, and **com**memorate **George Herbert and William** Cowper—

both religious poets, both Westminster scholars—and especially two opposite poles of the English Church—George Herbert, the 'ecclesiastical,' and William Cowper, the 'evangelical,' tendency. In the Window, Herbert is represented in his clerical vesture, standing by his Church porch, and the lines underneath are taken from the introduction to his poems, and (in reference to the Baptistery, or the entrance to the Abbey) touch at the start on the Christian life. Cowper, on the other side, is in his well-known cap and dressing-gown, in the neighborhood of Olney, with his hares in the garden, looking at his 'Mother's Picture,' from which poem are taken the lines which are also appropriate to the associations of the Baptistery. The heraldic devices above represent their respective families—both, as it happens, great in the English aristocracy."

The editor of 'Sunday at Home' added to the good Dean's note that "it was a happy thought of Dean Stanley to associate the names in the Memorial, and the gift of the Window was a fitting and graceful tribute from an American citizen in the Centennial Year of Independence."

THE ABBEY A BOND OF UNION.

From a private letter to MR. CHILDS written by a distinguished man of letters in England, and referring to the death of Dean Stanley, the following interesting extracts are made: "The good Dean valued your friendship deeply, and I have often heard him speak with enthusiasm of your affection for England and the Abbey, and the munificently splendid way in which you showed it. I have no doubt that the recollection by you of the truly kind and genial reception which you gave him in Philadelphia will remain with you as one of the brightest incidents of your life." The writer, referring to Dr. Bradley, who succeeded Dr. Stanley as Dean of Westminster, says: "He is a man who will not fail to carry on the work at Westminster thoroughly in the Stanleyian spirit, though, of course, no one can rival our dear Dean in gifts and energy. But you and all Stanley's American friends may rest assured that the tradition which you have all associated with the Abbey for so many years will still be maintained, and that the Abbey will remain during Bradley's deanery a bond of union between the two countries as it was in Stanley's time."

A REMINDER OF HOME.

In W. W. Nevin's entertaining 'Vignettes of Travel' there occurs the following reference to Mr. Childs's gift to the Abbey:—

"Passing from the ancient abbot's palace, now the dwelling of the Dean, by private entrance to the church, just before we entered the transept of the main building, Dean Stanley, to whom my presence started recollections of Philadelphia, said, 'Stop a moment; I want to show you something that will remind you of home,' and ascending by a side entry three narrow steps, into a little chapel shut off by an open railing from public entrance, we stood suddenly before the handsome Memorial Window of Mr. Childs to the two English poets—a grand blaze of illumination, covering almost an entire wall of the chapel. It is a beautiful and costly work of art, in the conventional ecclesiastical style of glass-painting, rich and impressive.

"It is the usage of the Abbey to inscribe on all monuments the incidents of their erection, but the story of this one is very simply and frankly told in a single line: 'D. D.* Georgius Gulielmus Childs. Civis Americanus.'

---

* Donum dedit.

"This is the first appearance of our country in the historic Abbey. There are a few other American names—some Royal refugees in the War of 1776-83, some colonial worthies, some British soldiers killed in the Revolution and French Wars; but this is the only description which distinctly places the new nation of 'The United States of America' in the monumental archives of Westminster."

IMPRESSIONS OF AN AMERICAN VISITOR TO THE ABBEY.

Mr. Joel Cook, in his entertaining book, entitled 'A Holiday Tour in Europe,' says, regarding the gift of MR. CHILDS: "The Memorial Window erected by MR. GEORGE W. CHILDS is eagerly sought for by Americans visiting the Abbey. . . . MR. CHILDS's gift is in two parts, or, as it were, two complete Windows, one in memory of Herbert and the other of Cowper. It is the extreme western window on the south side of the nave, and is in the Baptistery, somewhat secluded on account of the high tombs standing in front of it, and the stone arched railing separates the Baptistery from the nave, but pouring a rich flood of mellow light over them."

THE MILTON WINDOW

IN

ST. MARGARET'S CHURCH, WESTMINSTER.

THE MILTON WINDOW.

THE gift by Mr. George W. Childs to St. Margaret's Church, Westminster, of the Memorial Window to Milton was made subsequently to that of the Fountain, commemorative of Shakspeare, at Stratford-upon-Avon, and was inspired by a letter to him from the Venerable Archdeacon Farrar, in which was regretfully recited the absence of any appropriate memorial in England to the great Cromwellian poet, except that erected in 1737 by Auditor Benson in Westminster Abbey. To this letter its recipient at once replied by offering to place in St. Margaret's Church, of which the Venerable Archdeacon is Rector, a window, the design of which should be determined wholly by the judgment of the latter, Mr. Childs's only request to his friend being that he should undertake the setting up of a monument which should appropriately commemorate the virtues and genius of Milton, whose works are held in as great esteem, and whose memory is as profoundly reverenced in this country, as in that of his birth. The suggestion which came to MR. CHILDS was in harmony with the sentiment which had induced the presentation of the Memorial of Herbert and Cowper in Westminster Abbey, and the Fountain at Stratford-upon-Avon of Shakspeare, which were to serve as a sign of the appreciation in America of the genius of the poets to whom they were dedicated, and to give assurance to the world of the warmth of the affection and the sincerity of the esteem existing in the United States for these great masters of English literature, who embellished and ennobled our common language by their contributions to it.

ST. MARGARET'S CHURCH.

"London and Westminster," says old Heywood, "are two twin-sister cities, as joined by one street, so watered by one stream; the first a breeder of grave magistrates; the second the burial-place of great monarchs". St. Margaret's Church is in

Westminster, standing hard by the stately Abbey. The present sacred edifice indicates no earlier period of its existence than that of the reign of the Plantagenets; but Mr. Mackenzie Walcott says of it: "There is, with the exception of the Abbey of St. Peter and St. Paul's Cathedral, no other ecclesiastical edifice throughout London and Westminster which can boast of a greater antiquity, or more interesting foundation," the original structure dating, it is stated, from a few years before the Conquest. One story of its origin is to the effect that, "Edward, the Confessor, finding, as was natural, that a population was growing up around the Abbey walls, and was continually increased further by a miscellaneous crowd of persons, who, for good or for bad reasons, sought the shelter of the Sanctuary, raised here a church in the round-arched Saxon style, and dedicated it to St. Margaret."

In the reign of Edward the First the edifice was almost wholly taken down and rebuilt. There are some notable tombs in St. Margaret's Church, among others that to William Caxton, "who, as early as the year 1477, set up a printing-press in the Abbey; there is also a mural tablet set up within which recites that Sir Walter Raleigh's body was buried here on the day of his execution in Palace Yard."

Until very recently the Speaker and the House of Commons were wont to attend at St. Margaret's Church upon the days of what were known as the "State Services." In 1858 these were, by an order in Council, stricken out of the Book of Common Prayer, and since then the Speaker has not appeared in St. Margaret's in his official wig and robes.

In the year 1656 John Milton was married to his second wife, Catherine Woodcock, in St. Margaret's Church, and there he subsequently worshiped.

It may be proper to note here that, as a token of the high appreciation of Mr. Childs's gift to St. Margaret's, there has been set apart in perpetuity in that sacred temple a pew for the exclusive use of Americans.

It was in the latter part of 1886 that Archdeacon Farrar originally referred to the pitiful lack of imposing monuments to the Poet Milton in England. It was then that he wrote the following lines, with which he concluded his interesting article entitled "The Share of America in Westminster Abbey," before referred to in these pages, and which were published in 'Harper's Magazine' more than a year afterwards:—

"There are, perhaps, fewer memorials of Milton than of any Englishman of the same transcendent greatness. I am extremely desirous to erect a worthy Window in his honor in the Church of St. Margaret's, close beside the Abbey. Our register contains the record of his marriage to Catherine Woodcock, his second wife, in 1656, and also records, in the following year, her death and that of her infant daughter. It was to her that he addressed the noble sonnet which begins:—

> 'Methought I saw my late espoused saint
> Come to me like Alcestis from the grave.'

Milton's connection with the Church of St. Margaret's was therefore very close, and if any of his American admirers are willing to assist me in my design, I shall on public grounds most heartily welcome their munificence. They have already beautified this fine old historic Church by their splendid gift of a Window in honor of Sir Walter Raleigh, whose headless body lies under the altar. Milton has even higher claims on their gratitude and admiration."

This, in effect, was the text of the letter which was written by the Venerable Archdeacon to MR. CHILDS in November, 1886, and to which the latter replied by offering to contribute such a memorial as his friend should deem appropriate.

The other letters which have come into the Editor's possession having reference to the Milton Window are the following: the first is from Archdeacon Farrar to MR. CHILDS, dated at Dean's Yard, Westminster, London, February 4, 1887 :—

"MY DEAR MR. CHILDS :—

"I did not write *at once* to express my delight and heartfelt gratitude for your splendidly munificent offer in compliance with my suggestion of a Memorial to John Milton, because I wanted to give you full particulars. I did not say that Milton himself was buried at St. Margaret's, but that he was *married* in the Church, was closely connected with it through the Parliament (for it is and always has been the Church of the House of Commons), and that his dearest wife, the one to whom he wrote the immortal sonnet which begins—

'Methought I saw my late espoused saint'—

was buried in the Church, as was his child, wholly without memorial. The fact is that no man of his pure and noble genius is so wholly uncommemorated in England. There is a poor bust to him in the Abbey, that is all. For one hundred and fifty years after his **death** the Stuart reaction against Puritanism and the adoration of 'King Charles the Martyr' caused Milton's name to be execrated. But America is the glorious child of Puritanism; and it is to me a most touching and significant fact that a Memorial to Milton in the Church of the House of Commons for which he so greatly labored should now be given by a descendant of the Pilgrim Fathers after I had tried in vain to get it from Englishmen.

"But I could not write till I was able to inform you what the cost would be, nor shall I formally accept your generous offer until you have been informed of the cost and character of the proposed Window. The central compartments would illustrate scenes in the Life of Milton, the side compartments would contain scenes from the 'Paradise Lost.' The Window would be worthy of Milton, worthy of the church, and worthy of your munificence.

"I shall not set the artist to work till I receive your sanction in another letter. If you approve, I will have a fine design of the Window executed and sent to you. Mr. J. R. Lowell wrote the lines under the Raleigh Window in my church, and Lord Tennyson those under the Caxton Window. I would get some great poet to write the lines under the inscription which would record, to all future time, your honor of the illustrious dead.

"I have of course not mentioned the matter publicly, nor will I do so till I receive the final notification of your gift.

"Most gratefully and sincerely yours,

"F. W. FARRAR.

"P. S.—Immediately after writing this letter I went to read prayers, and the lesson was the message to the Angel of the Church of Philadelphia."

The following is Mr. Childs's reply to the foregoing:—

"PHILADELPHIA, February 16, 1887.

"MY DEAR ARCHDEACON FARRAR:—

"Your kind note is just received, and is most satisfactory. I have but one thought with regard to the Memorial, which is that I am particularly anxious you should write the inscription. All other matters I leave to your taste and good judgment, but this one request I hope you will grant me.

"With cordial regards, sincerely your friend,

"GEO. W. CHILDS."

Enclosed in the foregoing letter from Mr. Childs

was a draft for an amount covering the entire cost of the work.

Writing to his friend from Dean's Yard, Westminster, London, on the 5th day of March following, Archdeacon Farrar said:—

"My Dear Mr. Childs:—

"How can I thank you warmly enough? Your order for £—— has reached me safely, and the Window, which will be a very beautiful one, will be at once proceeded with. Before long I hope to send you a painting of it which will show you how very beautiful it is likely to be. I need hardly say that, as you wish it, I will myself write the inscription, and, further, I shall record that it is the gift of the same noble munificence which has already enriched Westminster Abbey and Stratford-upon-Avon.

"I wish that there were some chance of your seeing it! Of course, it will take some months to finish, and may be you will have to come over to England some day, before or after the Memorial is set up.

"You cannot tell how much I am pleased by the thought that one of the greatest, purest, and least commemorated of English poets should receive one more testimony to the immortal gratitude which is his due, and that the Memorial to this mighty Puritan should come from the land of the Pilgrim Fathers, and be placed in the Church of the House of Commons, with which he was so closely connected.

"Believe me to be, dear MR. CHILDS, sincerely and gratefully, your friend,

"F. W. FARRAR."

On the 19th day of the same month Archdeacon Farrar again wrote to MR. CHILDS, from Dean's Yard, Westminster, regarding the Window, as follows:—

"MY DEAR MR. CHILDS:—

"I hope, in the course of a few weeks, to send you a beautifully painted copy of the design for the great Milton Window which we owe to your munificence. When the design is completed, I shall publicly announce your gift to the old historic church. The enclosed outline will give you a general conception of the mode of treatment. In the centre is Milton dictating to his daughter the 'Paradise Lost'; underneath is a scene from his student-life, and his visit to Galileo. All around are scenes from 'Paradise Lost' and 'Paradise Regained.' Above are the rejoicing angels, and figures of Adam and of our Lord. It will be a very beautiful work of art, and an eternal monument to Milton's genius and your generosity.

"Believe me to be, dear MR. CHILDS, sincerely and gratefully your friend,

"F. W. FARRAR."

THE WINDOW UNVEILED.

The gift of MR. CHILDS was formally unveiled on the eighteenth day of February, 1888, an account of which was furnished by Archdeacon Farrar himself in the following letter to the donor:—

"17 DEAN'S YARD, WESTMINSTER, S. W.
"February 18, 1888.

"MY DEAR MR. CHILDS:—

"I have just returned from the unveiling of the Milton Window. I only invited a select number of friends. Among those present were the poets Mr. Robert Browning and Mr. Lewis Morris, among others Mr. Lecky, Mr. Courtney Herbert, Mr. and the Baroness Burdett-Coutts, the Speaker's family, the United States Minister and Mrs. Phelps, Professor and Mrs. Flower, Lord Stanley of Alderly,

General Sir Edward Staveley, and other distinguished personages. Mr. Matthew Arnold read a very fine paper on Milton, which is to be published in the 'Century,' and which will, I am sure, please you very much. After the paper had been read in the Vestry we went into the Church and unveiled the Window. It is very fine in color and execution. In the centre is Milton dedicating to his daughters the 'Paradise Lost;' below is Milton as a boy at St. Paul's school, and Milton visiting Galileo. All round are scenes from the 'Paradise Lost'—Satan awaking his legion, Satan entering Paradise, the fall, and the expulsion from Eden. Above are four scenes from the 'Paradise Regained'—the nativity, the annunciation, the baptism of Christ, and the temptation in the wilderness. At the top are jubilant angels, and Adam and our Lord, the first and the second Adam. In the course of next week I hope to send you the picture (colored) of the Window. Underneath is the inscription:

'To the Glory of God, and in memory of the Immortal Poet, John Milton, whose wife and child lie buried here, this Window is dedicated by GEORGE W. CHILDS of Philadelphia, MDCCCLXXXVIII.'

"On the other side are Mr. Whittier's four fine lines.

"So that now, my dear MR. CHILDS, your noble

gift has come to fruitful completion, and in the Church of the House of Commons will be a lasting and beautiful Memorial both of the great poet and of your munificence.

"It has carried out a wish which I long cherished. Heartfelt thanks!

"I shall preach on Milton to-morrow, and I shall ask you to accept the MS. of the sermon. Pray give my kindest remembrances to Mrs. Childs, and believe me to be,

"Yours, very sincerely and gratefully,
"F. W. FARRAR."

The selection of St. Margaret's Church was probably due to the fact mentioned in this letter, that Milton's wife and child are buried there, and what more fitting memorial could there be than this of him who in his 'Il Penseroso' wrote of

"Storied windows richly dight
Casting a dim religious light"?

MATTHEW ARNOLD'S ADDRESS.

The following is the complete text of the late Matthew Arnold's address, delivered in St. Margaret's Church, Westminster, on the 18th day of

February, 1888, on the occasion of the unveiling of the Memorial Window, being the same which is referred to by Archdeacon Farrar in the foregoing letter to MR. CHILDS:—

"The most eloquent voice of our century uttered, shortly before leaving the world, a warning cry against 'the Anglo-Saxon contagion.' The tendencies and aims, the view of life and the social economy, of the ever-multiplying and spreading Anglo-Saxon race, would be found congenial, this prophet feared, by all the prose, all the vulgarity amongst mankind, and would invade and overpower all nations. The true ideal would be lost, a general sterility of mind and heart would set in.

"The prophet had in view, no doubt, in the warning thus given, us and our colonies, but the United States still more. There the Anglo-Saxon race is already most numerous, there it increases fastest; there material interests are more absorbing and pursued with most energy; there the ideal, the saving ideal, of a high and rare excellence seems, perhaps, to suffer most danger of being obscured and lost. Whatever one may think of the general danger to the world from the Anglo-Saxon contagion, it appears to me difficult to deny that the growing greatness and influence of the United States does bring with it some danger to the ideal of a high and rare excellence. The *average man* is too much a religion there; his performance is unduly magnified, his shortcomings are not duly seen and admitted. A lady in the State of Ohio sent to me, only the other day, a **volume on** American authors; **the** praise given throughout was of such high pitch that in thanking her I could not forbear say**ing** that for only one or two of the authors named was such a strain of praise admissible, and that we lost all real standard of excellence by praising so uniformly and immoderately. She answered me, with charming good temper, that very likely **I was** quite right, but it was pleasant to her to think that excellence was common and abundant. But excellence is not common and abundant; on the contrary, **as the** Greek poet long ago said, excellence dwells among rocks hardly accessible, and a man must always wear his heart out before he can reach her. Whoever talks of excellence as common and abundant is on the way to lose all right standard of excellence. And when the right standard of excellence is lost, **it** is not likely that much which is excellent will **be** produced.

" To habituate ourselves, therefore, to approve, as the Bible says, things that are really excellent, is of the highest importance. And some apprehension may justly be caused by a tendency in Americans to take, or at any rate attempt to take, profess to take, the average man and his performances too seriously, to over-rate and over-praise what is not really superior.

"But we have met here to-day to witness the unveiling of a gift in Milton's honor, and a gift bestowed by an American, Mr. Childs of Philadelphia, whose cordial hospitality so many Englishmen, I myself among the number, have experienced in America. It was only last autumn that Stratford-upon-Avon celebrated the reception of a gift from the same generous donor in honor of Shakspeare. Shakspeare and Milton—he who wishes to keep his standard of excellence high cannot choose two better objects of regard and honor. And it is an American who has chosen them, and whose beautiful gift in honor of one of them, Milton, with Mr. Whittier's simple and true lines inscribed upon it, is unveiled to-day. Perhaps this gift in honor of Milton, of which I am asked to speak, is, even more than the gift in honor of Shakspeare, one to suggest edifying reflections to us.

"Like Mr. Whittier, I treat the gift of Mr. Childs as a gift in honor of Milton, although the Window given is in memory of the second wife, Catherine Woodcock, the 'late espoused saint' of the famous sonnet, who died in child-bed at the end of the first year of her marriage with Milton, and who lies buried here with her infant. Milton is buried in Cripplegate, but he lived for a good while in this parish of St. Margaret's, Westminster, and here he composed part of 'Paradise Lost,' and the whole of 'Paradise Regained' and 'Samson Agonistes.' When death deprived him of the Catherine whom the new Window commemorates, Milton had still some eighteen years to live, and Cromwell, his 'chief of men,' was yet ruling England. But the Restoration, with its 'Sons of Belial,' was not far off; and in the mean time Milton's heavy affliction had laid fast hold upon him, his eyesight had failed totally, he was blind. In what remained to him of life he had the consolation of producing the 'Paradise Lost' and the 'Samson Agonistes,' and such a consolation we may indeed count as no slight one. But the daily life of happiness in common things and in domestic affections—a life of which, to Milton as to Dante, too small a share was given—he seems to have known most, if not only, in his one married year with the wife who is here buried. Her form 'vested all in white,' as in his sonnet he relates that after her death she appeared to him, her face veiled, but, with 'love, sweetness, and goodness' shining in her person—this fair and gentle daughter of the rigid sectarist of Hackney, this lovable companion with whom Milton had rest and happiness one year, is a part of Milton indeed, and in calling up her memory we call up his.

"And in calling up Milton's memory we call up, let me say, a memory upon which, in prospect of the Anglo-Saxon contagion and of its dangers supposed and real, it may be well to lay stress even more than upon Shakspeare. If to our English race an inadequate sense for perfection of work is a real danger, if the discipline of respect for a high and flawless excellence is peculiarly needed by us, Milton is of all our gifted men the best lesson, the most salutary influence. In the sure and flawless perfection of his rhythm and diction he is as admirable as Virgil or Dante, and in this respect he is unique amongst us. No one else in English literature and art possesses the like distinction.

"Thomson, Cowper, Wordsworth, all of them good poets who have studied Milton, followed Milton, adopted his form, fail in their diction and rhythm if we try them by that high standard of excellence maintained by Milton constantly. From style really high and pure Milton never departs; their departures from it are frequent.

"Shakspeare is divinely strong, right, and attractive. But sureness of perfect style Shakspeare himself does not possess. I have heard a politician express wonder at the treasures of political wisdom in a certain celebrated **scene of** 'Troilus and Cressida;' for my part I am at least equally moved to wonder at the fantastic and false diction **in** which Shakspeare has in that scene clothed them. Milton, from one end of 'Paradise Lost' to the other, is in his diction and rhythm constantly a great artist in the great style. Whatever may be said **as to the** subject of his poem, as to the conditions under which he received his subject and treated it, that praise, at any rate, is assured to him.

"For the rest, justice is not at present done, **in** my opinion, **to** Milton's management of the inevitable matter of a Puritan epic, a matter full of difficulties for a poet. Justice is not done to the *architectonics*, as Goethe would have called them, of 'Paradise Lost;' in these, too, the power of Milton's art is remarkable. But this may be **a** proposition which requires discussion and development for establishing it, and they are impossible on an occasion like the present.

"That Milton, of all our English **race**, is by his

diction and rhythm the one artist of the highest rank in the great style whom we have; this I take as requiring no discussion, this I take as certain.

"The mighty power of poetry and art is generally admitted. But where the soul of this power, of this power at its best, chiefly resides, very many of us fail to see. It resides chiefly in the refining and elevation wrought in us by the high and rare excellence of the great style. We may feel the effect without being able to give ourselves clear account of its cause, but the thing is so. Now, no race needs the influences mentioned, the influences of refining and elevation, more than ours; and in poetry and art our grand source for them is Milton.

"To what does he owe this supreme distinction? To nature first and foremost, to that bent of nature for inequality which, to the worshipers of the average man, is so unacceptable; to a gift, a divine favor. 'The older one grows,' says Goethe, 'the more one prizes natural gifts, because by no possibility can they be procured and stuck on.' Nature formed Milton to be a great poet. But what other poet has shown so sincere a sense of the grandeur of his vocation, and a moral effort so constant and sublime to make and keep himself worthy of it? The Milton of religious and political controversy,

and perhaps of domestic life also, is not seldom disfigured by want of amenity, by acerbity. **The Mil**ton of poetry, on the other hand, is one of those great men 'who are modest'—to quote a fine remark of Leopardi, that gifted and stricken young Italian, who, in his sense for poetic style, is worthy to be named with Dante and Milton—'who are modest, **because** they continually compare themselves, not **with** other men, but with that idea of the perfect which they have before their mind.' The Milton of poetry is the man, in his own magnificent phrase, of 'devout prayer to that Eternal **Spirit** that can enrich with all utterance and knowledge, and sends out his Seraphim with the hallowed fire of his altar to touch and purify the lips of whom he pleases.' And, **finally,** the Milton of poetry is, in his own words again, the man of 'industrious and select reading.' Continually **he** lived in companionship with high and rare excellence, **with** the great Hebrew poets and prophets, with the great poets of Greece and Rome. The Hebrew compositions were not in verse, and can be not inadequately represented by **the** grand measured prose of our English **Bible.** The verse of the poets of Greece and Rome no translation can adequately reproduce. Prose cannot have the power of verse; verse translation may give whatever of charm is in the soul and talent of the **translator** himself, but never the specific charm of **the verse and** poet translated. **In our race are** thousands **of** readers, presently there will be millions, who know not a word of Greek and Latin, and will never learn those languages. If this host of readers are ever to gain any sense of the power and charm of the great poets of antiquity, their way to gain it is not through translations of the ancients, but through the original poetry of Milton, who has the like power and charm, because he has the like great style.

"Through **Milton they** may gain it, for, in conclusion, Milton is English; this **master in the** great style of the ancients is English. Virgil, whom Milton loved **and** honored, has at the end of the 'Æneid' a noble passage, where Juno, seeing the **defeat** of Turnus and **the** Italians imminent, the victory of the Trojan invaders assured, entreats Jupiter that Italy may nevertheless survive and be herself still, **may** retain her own mind, manners, and language, and not adopt those of the conqueror.

'Sit Latium, sint Albani per secula rages!'

Jupiter grants the prayer; he promises perpetuity and the future to Italy—Italy re-enforced by whatever virtue the Trojan race has, but Italy, not Troy.

This we may take as a sort of parable suiting ourselves. All the Anglo-Saxon contagion, all the flood of Anglo-Saxon commonness, beats vainly against the great style, but cannot shake it, and has to accept its triumph. But it triumphs in Milton, in one of our own race, tongue, faith, and morals. Milton has made the great style no longer an exotic here; he has made it an inmate amongst us, a leaven, and a power. Nevertheless, he, and his hearers on both sides of the Atlantic, are English and will remain English :—

'Sermonem Ausonii patrium moresque tenebunt.'

The English race overspreads the world, and at the same time the ideal of an excellence the most high and the most rare abides a possession with it forever."

The foregoing address was published in 'The Century Magazine' for May, 1888.

HIS LAST WORK.

This noble tribute to Milton was the last work which this learned and graceful scholar lived to do. A short time after its delivery Dr. Arnold died.

The following letter from Archdeacon Farrar to Mr. Childs will be found interesting in its reference to the final literary effort of the great scholar and divine:—

"ATHENÆUM CLUB, PALL MALL, S. W.,
"May 1, 1888.

"MY DEAR MR. CHILDS:—

"I felt Mr. Matthew Arnold's death deeply. He died on a Sunday, and only the Friday before he had been talking to me here at the Athenæum in the very highest spirits. He had alluded to the Milton Article (which has since appeared, a posthumous work). It will be interesting to you to know that it was called forth by your noble gift, and that it was the *last* thing which came from that brilliant intellect. I took part in his funeral at the quiet little village church of Laleham, where we laid him beside his three boys—two of whom had been my pupils at Harrow.

"The Window is beautiful. It will be a permanent and historic ornament to the Church, which will now have a record of your generosity as well as Westminster Abbey, where only yesterday I was reading the plate which commemorates your gift of the Cowper and Herbert Window.

"Cordially and sincerely yours,

"F. W. FARRAR."

DESCRIPTION OF THE WINDOW.

The Window is remarkable for its fulness of detail and richness of color. Both in artistic design and execution it is worthy of high praise. It is divided by its stone work into four lights with tracery openings, and is of fifteenth century character, known as the "perpendicular" style, which is that of the church generally. The design of the stained glass filling the Window in memory of the author of 'Paradise Lost' is planned on three lines of panels in horizontal order, the middle tier being of somewhat larger depth than those above and below it. In the two divisions of the central portions of the whole, four panels— viz., those of the central and lower tiers respectively of these lights—are devoted to the personal history of the poet. In one of the bottom panels the boy Milton is shown at St. Paul's school among his fellow-schoolmates. In the next panel Milton's visit to Galileo is depicted. Above these are two of the larger panels combined to make one central subject representing the poet dictating 'Paradise Lost' to his daughters. Around these panels are eight others illustrative of 'Paradise Lost' and 'Paradise Regained.'

In reference to the former are represented the incidents of: 1. Satan's summons to his legions. 2. Adam and Eve at prayer in Paradise, Satan looking on. 3. The temptation. 4. The expulsion. In the upper tier the four panels are devoted to the illustration respectively of: 1. The annunciation. 2. The nativity of our Lord. 3. The baptism of our Lord. 4. The defeat of Satan in his temptations of our Lord. In the tracery openings are jubilant angels and at the apex of the whole figures of Adam on the left and our Lord on the right, representing thus the first and second Adam respectively. At the base of the window is the following inscription:—

"To the Glory of God: and in memory of the immortal poet, John Milton: whose wife and child lie buried here: this window is dedicated by GEORGE W. CHILDS, of Philadelphia, MDCCCLXXXVIII."

Occupying a corresponding space and position in the window is the following fine verse thereon emblazoned, which was especially written for the Memorial by the American Quaker Poet, John Greenleaf Whittier, as a tribute to his brother Poet of long ago:—

"The New World honors him whose lofty plea
  For England's freedom made her own more sure,
Whose song, immortal as its theme, shall be
  Their common freehold while both worlds endure."

Regarding these lines **Mr.** Whittier wrote **to**
Mr. Childs as follows :—

"My Dear Friend :—

"I am glad to comply with thy request and that of our friend Archdeacon Farrar. I hope the lines may be satisfactory. It is difficult to put all that could be said of Milton in four lines. How very beautiful and noble thy benefactions are! Every one is a testimony of peace and good-will.

"I am, with high respect and esteem, thy aged friend,

"JOHN G. WHITTIER."

"I think even such a scholar as Dr. Farrar will not object to my use of the word 'freehold.' Milton himself uses it in the same way in his prose writings, viz. :—

"'I too have my chapter and *freehold* of rejoicing.'"

The religious services were the ordinary Lenten ones, except that the hymn preceding the sermon was Milton's:

"Let us with a gladsome mind,
Praise the Lord, for he is kind."

"Archdeacon Farrar, who preached from Lamentations iv. 7, emphasized the occasion in his opening remarks. While justly claiming attention to the fact that he never neglected to preach according to the church's season, year after year, through both the gloom and the glory of the Christian calendar, it had been and would be his endeavor to dwell with the congregation upon each sacred anniversary as it recurred, but he plainly announced on this occasion a departure from the usual practice, deferring for a week the usual Lenten exhortation. He devoted almost the whole address to pointing out the concrete lesson of Christianity as expounded by the noble life of Milton. A spontaneous, generous, and just expression of approval of the action of the donor of the Memorial Window was succeeded by an eloquent and keenly appreciative *résumé* of Milton's life as a Christian man, coupled with an unstinted tribute to his genius as a poet who derived inspiration from a divine source.

"As the discourse proceeded and the congregation warmed in sympathy with the impassioned but well-weighed eloquence of the preacher, the gloomy weather without cleared, and the wintry sun gleamed through the richly-stained windows with which St. Margaret's is generally adorned and glinted on the Milton Memorial, relieving the semi-obscurity of the interior and illuming the impressive scene in which the worshipers mingled with devotion to the Almighty the full meed of admiration of Milton's inspired genius which the preacher's fervency demanded."

THE SERVICES.

On the Sunday following the unveiling of the memorial to the poet, Archdeacon Farrar, in order to give greater impressiveness to the event, preached a special sermon in St. Margaret's. The day was bitterly cold, the wind blowing sharply from the northeast, and the snow falling intermittently during the morning; but, undeterred by the churlish weather, a vast multitude, including many of the most distinguished religious, social, political, and literary leaders of England, went to listen to the eloquent words of the Venerable Archdeacon. The pews were all filled, and chairs were placed in the aisles to accommodate the great concourse assembled to testify by their presence their interest in the impressive ceremony. Among those who were in attendance were Mr. Phelps, the American Minister, and his wife; Matthew Arnold; the poet, Robert Browning; the Baroness Burdett-Coutts; the Rev. Phillips Brooks, of Boston; and many prominent American residents of London, as well as distinguished representatives of the nobility.

The following is the full text of the sermon:—

"Her Nazarites were purer than snow, they were whiter than milk, they were more ruddy in body than rubies, their polishing was of sapphire.—LAM. iv. 7.

"This is the First Sunday in Lent, and you, my friends, will bear witness that I never neglect to preach on the Church's seasons. Year after year, through the gloom and glad of the calendar, from the splendor of the Nativity to the solemn shadows of Passion Week, it has been said—and, God helping me, it will be—my endeavor to dwell with you upon the lessons of each sacred anniversary. Naturally to-day I should have striven to remind you of the deep meaning of Lent; and so I shall do, though less obviously than usual. Leaving till next Sunday the more direct treatment of that subject, to-day I would point to some of those lessons in the concrete, as exhibited in a noble life. And I would humbly pray you to listen without impatience or prejudice, for I shall enter into no disputable points, I shall try not to hurt any susceptibilities; I shall point only to that which was indisputably excellent in one who showed that temperance, soberness, and chastity which it is the very object of Lent to teach.

"It has been my desire during twelve **years to** surround this ancient and famous church with noble associations; to revive the memories of those great men with which it has been connected, and thus to indicate the relation in which it stands to the history of England.

"To commemorate events of recent days the **members of** the House of Commons, whose church it is, **have** erected the window which recalls **the** tragic death of Lord Frederick Cavendish; and memorials have been placed here to Lord Hatherly, the good Lord Chancellor; to Lord Farnborough, who spent his life in the service of Parliament; and **in token of** our gratitude for fifty years of almost unbroken pros**perity** under the reign of **a** beloved **Queen, the Caxton** window was given by the printers **of** London **in memory of** that great man who lies buried **here**; and citizens of America in their large-handed generosity **and care for** the great traditions which **are** their heritage **no less than** ours, have presented us with that brilliant west window, which commemorates nothing less than the founding of the New World.

"But this church may also claim its special interest in the mighty name of Milton. That name is **re**corded in our marriage register; and here lies buried, with Milton's infant daughter, that beloved wife—

'my late espoused saint'—whose love flung one brief gleam of happiness over the poet's troubled later years. Once more we are indebted to an American citizen for the beautiful Milton Window which was yesterday unveiled. The well-counselled munificence of Mr. CHILDS, of Philadelphia, who has already enriched Stratford-upon-Avon with a memorial of Shakspeare, and Westminster Abbey with the Window in memory of Herbert and Cowper, has now erected this abiding memorial to the great Puritan Poet. Myself the debtor to American friends for great kindness, I cannot but rejoice that the Church of St. Margaret's should furnish yet one more illustration of those bonds of common traditions and blood and language and affection which unite England to the great Republic of the West; and I am glad that the public spirit of the church-wardens has assigned from henceforth the use of one special pew in this church to our friends and visitors from the other side of the Atlantic.

"There was something specially appropriate in the Milton Window being the gift of an American. For the United States represent much that Milton most deeply loved; the commonwealth which, happily failing in England, in America gloriously succeeded; the Puritanism which, crushed in England, inspired vigor and nobleness into our kin beyond the sea. 'Paradise Lost' was the one English poem which the sons of the Pilgrim Fathers loved. Until Longfellow inspired New England with a fresh sense of the sacredness of art and song, that poem alone tempered with the colorings of imagination the stern Hebrew ideal bequeathed to their descendants by those who sailed in the Mayflower.

"And some of Milton's most honored friends were closely connected with America. The younger Sir Henry Vane, to whom he addressed the sonnet,

> 'Vane, young in years, but in sage counsel old,'

Vane, who has been called 'one of the greatest and purest men who ever walked the earth to adorn and elevate his kind,' emigrated to New England in 1635, and was elected governor in 1636. Of Roger Williams, 'the apostle of soul freedom,' the founder of Rhode Island, Milton speaks as 'that extraordinary man and most enlightened legislator, who, after suffering persecutions from his brethren, persevered amid incredible hardships and difficulties in seeking a place of refuge for the sacred ark of freedom;' and Roger Williams, in a letter to Governor Winthrop, kindly communicated to me by his descendant, the Hon. R. C. Winthrop, of Boston, says, 'The secretary of the council, Mr. Milton, for my Dutch I read him, read me many more languages.'

"The venerable poet, Mr. Whittier, who has written the lines for yonder window, most justly says:—

> 'The New World honors him whose lofty plea
> For England's freedom made her own more sure,
> Whose song, immortal as its theme, shall be
> Their common freehold while both worlds endure.'

"1. I propose this morning to speak to you about Milton; not, of course, in the political aspect of his life, and still less by way of criticising his poems, but as a man of uniquely noble personality, who, whatever may have been his other errors, set to the world an example of godly life which is supremely needed in the present day. 'Character,' says Emerson, 'is higher than intellect,' and a great writer has said of Milton that 'it may be doubted whether any man was altogether so great, taking into our view at once his manly virtue, his superhuman genius, his zeal for truth (for true patriotism, true freedom), his eloquence in displaying it, his contempt for personal power, his glory and exultation in his country's.' Were I to search the whole range of English history for a type of Christian nobleness, who might inspire our youths with the glory of a distinguished life, and the magnanimity of a lofty character, I know no one in whom was better manifested the indefinable distinction, the life-long self-restraint, the intense purpose, the grave self-respect, the lofty disdain for all which was sordid and ignoble which marks the sincerity of the sons of God. He was, as Wordsworth says of him:—

> 'Soul awful—if this world has ever held
> An awful soul.'

"2. Of these four great cardinal virtues into which virtue has been divided since moral philosophy began—prudence, temperance, fortitude, and justice—the first three are pre-eminently virtues which Lent should evoke, and they shone conspicuously in the life of Milton. Take his youth. What a lesson is conveyed to the mental indolence of the mass of ordinary English boys by the ardor of this glorious young student, who, at the age of twelve, when he was at St. Paul's School, learned with such eagerness that he scarcely ever went to bed before midnight. He tells us that even in early years he took labor and intent study to be his portion in this life. While he could write Latin like a Roman, he had also mastered Greek, French, Italian, Syriac, and Hebrew.

"Do not imagine that, therefore, he was some pallid student or stunted ascetic. On the contrary he was a boy full of force and fire, full of self-control, eminently beautiful, eminently pure, a good fencer, an accomplished swordsman, and this young and holy student would probably have defeated in every manly exercise a dozen of the youths who have nothing to be proud of save their ignorance and their vices—the dissipated loungers and oglers at refreshment bars, who need perpetual glasses of ardent spirits to support their wasted energies. In him the sound body was the fair temple of a lovely soul. And even while we watch him as a youth we see the two chief secrets of his grandeur. The first was his exquisite purity. From earliest years he thought himself a fit person to do the noblest and godliest deeds and far better worth than to deject and debase by such a defilement as sin is, himself so highly ransomed and ennobled to friendship and filial relation with God. From the first he felt that every free and gentle spirit, even without the oath of knighthood, was born a knight, nor needed to expect the gilt spurs nor the laying a sword upon his shoulder to stir him up both by his counsel and his arms to protect the weakness of chastity.

"From the first he cherished within himself a certain high fastidiousness and virginal delicacy of soul, an honest haughtiness of modest self-esteem which made him shrink with the loathing of a youthful Joseph from coarse contaminations. He went to Christ's College, Cambridge, at the age of sixteen, and remained there seven years. Wordsworth, describing what he was as **a** youth at Cambridge, **says**:

'**I seem to** see him here familiarly, and in his scholar's dress bounding before me, yet a stripling youth:

> 'A boy, no better, with his rosy cheeks,
> Angelical, keen eye, courageous look,
> And conscious step of purity and pride.'

"The vulgar soul rarely loves the noble, **and it** was Milton's stainless chastity, together with his personal beauty, which gained him the name of '**the Lady,**' until the dislike of his meaner fellows gave way before his moral nobleness and intellectual prominence. What he was at that time may be seen in his earliest lines on the death of a fair infant,

'Soft, silken primrose fading timelessly,'

written when he was but seventeen. What his thoughts were we learn also from those autobiographic passages of his writings in which with a superb and ingenuous egotism **he** put to shame the foul slanders of his enemies. 'If,' he said, 'God ever instilled an intense love of moral beauty into the breast of any man, He has instilled it into mine.' It is in this purity of his ideal that he stands so far as a man above all that we know of Shakspeare. He could not because he would not have written much that Shakspeare wrote; still less would he have descended from that high place in which he sat with his garland and singing robes about him, to **mingle** with those other Elizabethan dramatists who

'Stood around
The throne of Shakspeare, sturdy but unclean.'

And had **the glorious** young Puritan ever **appeared** as **a** boy at one of the drinking bouts and wit encounters at **the** Mermaid Tavern, **and** propounded his grave theory that he who would be a true poet must aim first to make his **life** a true **poem, I think,** with his biographer, that a **blush may have** passed **over** the swarthy cheek of Ben Jonson, and that Shakspeare might have bent his head to hide a noble tear. Austere he was; **but** his was neither **the ab**sorbed austerity of the **scholar,** nor **the ostentatious** austerity of the Pharisee, **nor the** agonizing self-introspection **of a** monk, but the sweet and grave austerity of a hero and a sage.

"**And** the other youthful germ of his greatness

was his high steadfastness of purpose. Most men live only from hand to mouth. The bias of their life is prescribed to them by accident. They are driven hither and thither by the gusts of their own passions, or become the sport and prey of others, or intrust the decision of their course to the 'immoral god, circumstance.' In the words of Isaiah, 'Gad and Meni are the idols of their service; they prepare a table for chance and furnish a drink-offering to Destiny.' From such idols no inspiration comes. But Milton's mind, he tells us, was set wholly on the accomplishment of great designs. 'You ask me, Charles, of what I am thinking,' he wrote to his young friend and schoolfellow, Charles Diodati; 'I think, so help me Heaven, of immortality.' He had early learned 'to scorn delights, and live laborious days.' His whole youth—the six years at school, the seven years at Cambridge, the five of studious retirement at Horton—were all intended as one long preparation for the right use of those abilities which he regarded as 'the inspired gift of God rarely bestowed.' He felt that he who would be a true poet ought himself to be a true poem. He meant that the great poem which even then he meditated should be drawn 'neither from the heat of youth, or the vapors of wine, like that which flows at waste from the pen of some vulgar amourist or the trencher fury of some rhyming parasite, but by devout prayer to that Eternal Spirit, who can enrich with all utterance and knowledge, and sends out His seraphim with the hallowed fire of His altar, to touch and purify the lips of whom he pleases.'

"Poetry was not to him as to the roystering town-poets and love-poets and wit-poets of his times, the practice of a knack and the provision of an amusement, but he believed that the Holy Spirit to whom he devoutly prayed could help him by means of his verse to imbreed and cherish in a great people the deeds of virtue and public civility; to allay the perturbations of the mind and set the affections in right tune; to celebrate, in glorious and lofty hymns, the throne and equipage of God's Almightiness . . . . to sing victorious agonies of saints and martyrs, the deeds and triumphs of just and pious nations doing valiantly through faith against the enemies of Christ; to deplore the relapses of kingdoms and states from justice and God's true worship; lastly, whatsoever in religion is holy and sublime, in virtue amiable and grave, all these to paint and to describe.

"And as one means to the evolution of this poem, his

> 'Care was fixed and zealously intent
> To fill his odorous lamp with deeds of light
> And hope that reaps not shame.'

"Puritan he was. Yet there was nothing **sour or** fanatical in his Puritanism. He loved music, he loved art, he loved science, he loved the drama. And in these years he wrote Comus, which, amid its festal splendor and rural sweetness, is the loveliest poem ever written in praise of chastity; and Lycidas, in which we first see that terrible two-handed engine at the door, and hear the first mut**ters of** that storm which was to sweep so much **away.**

"3. In 1638 Milton started on his travels. **His** travels were not filled with inanities and debaucheries, as were those of too many. **In Paris he was** introduced to the great Hugo Grotius; **in Florence** to the 'Starry Galileo'; in Naples to the Marquis Manso, who had been the friend and patron of Tasso; **at** Rome his bold faithfulness brought him **into peril.** He had intended to proceed to Greece and Sicily, but the sad news of civil discord in England called him home. In those stern days men could not shilly-shally down the stream of popular compromise. They were forced to take a side, and Milton took his side against that which he regarded a feeble tyranny and ruthless priestcraft. 'When God,' he says, 'commands to take the trumpet and **blow a** dolorous and jarring blast, **it lies** not in man's will what he shall say or what he shall conceal. I considered it dishonorable to be enjoying myself in foreign lands, while my countrymen were striking a blow for freedom.' You may disapprove—you may honorably disapprove of the part he took. Remember only that on both sides in that great civil war in England were noble, righteous, and holy men; and that we, sitting in our arm-chairs, are hardly adequate to judge of the mighty issues of national life and death which were at stake in that tremendous conflict. Thus, then, ended the youth—the happy, pure, and noble youth of Milton.

"4. His manhood, from 1640–1660, was a period of immense self-sacrifice. Laying aside, for a time, all his highest hopes, and leaving 'the calm and pleasing solitariness' wherein, amid cheerful thoughts, he could gaze on the bright countenance of truth in the still air of delightful studies, he was forced to embark on a troubled sea of noises and harsh disputes. If his arguments are 'flushed with passion;' if we regret some of his opinions and many of those vehemencies in which even the stout timbers of his native language seem to strain and crack under the Titanic force of his indignation, we must remember that amid domestic misery, fierce excitement, and a world of disesteem, it was the one passion of his life to defend liberty ('religious liberty against the prelates, civil liberty against the crown, the liberty of the press against the executive, the liberty of conscience, the liberty of domestic life'). The unparalleled splendor and majesty **of** those passages in his prose writings in which he soars above the clamors of controversy, show the holy seriousness of his **aims.** And besides these glorious pages, two of his **prose** writings are of permanent value. In the 'Areopagitica' he established the liberty of the press; **in** the 'Tractate on Education' his ideal is not **the** pelting and peddling ideal of finical pedagogues, but that large conception of teaching which shall enable a man to 'perform justly, skilfully, and magnanimously all offices, both public and private, of peace and war,' and 'to repair the ruin of our first parents **by** regaining to know God aright.' Even when he was threatened with blindness as the result of excessive labors in the public cause, 'the choice,' he says, 'lay before me, between dereliction of a supreme duty and loss of eyesight; I could not but obey that inward monitor, I know not what, that spake to me from heaven.' In 1653, at the age of forty-four, he became totally blind, and in 1656 his one brief gleam of domestic happiness, in his second marriage, was quenched forever by the death of that sweet wife, and that infant child, who lie buried here.

"5. So ended the manhood of storm and stress and passionate tumult, and then came the long, dark afternoon of his life, in the total ruin and eclipse of the cause which he had so passionately served. In 1660 Charles the Second was restored, and Milton was barely saved from imminent peril of death to be flung aside as a blind and hated outcast by a country which at once sank into the very nadir of its degradation. The Restoration was a hideous reaction of servility against all freedom, of impurity against all righteousness. Amid that bibulous dissonance of Bacchus and his revellers the one pure and lofty voice was drowned. In that orgy of drunkenness and license the high ideal of Milton was trampled as under the hoofs of swine. Who can think without a blush of moral cataclysm and conflagration in which debauchery rioted in high places unrebuked; in which adulterers and adulteresses thronged the desecrated chambers of Whitehall; in which a perjured trifler complacently pocketed the subsidies of France; in which the name of 'Saint' was regarded as the most crushing of all sarcasms, and the wittiest of all jibes; in which the nation's life was tainted through and through with vices; in which the purity of England withered like a garland in a Fury's breath, and her heroic age vanished 'not by gradual decay, not by imperceptible degeneracy, but like the winter snow at noon'? Some of us have known what is the anguish of watching in vain the stealthy growth of ignoble error; of taking the unpopular and the failing side; but scarcely one of us can imagine the colossal tragedy of Milton's trial. The Roman poet in his immortal line says:—

'Victrix causa Diis placuit, sed victa Catoni.'

"Yet the overthrow which Cato witnessed at Thapsus was nothing to the moral overthrow which Milton witnessed after 1660, and the suicide of Cato at Utica compared with Milton's patient endurance is as paganism is to Christianity. Amid a moral miasma deadlier than the great plague which drove him from London; amid conflagration of all things noble, more destructive than the great fire, in irretrievable discomfiture, standing utterly alone, blind, impoverished, hated, his friends dead, his hopes blasted, his dear ones lost, his children undutiful, his whole life's labor dashed into total shipwreck, and overwhelmed under the foul and crawling foam of an ignoble society—to one so circumstanced

'Among new men, strange faces, other minds,'

any amount of despair or prostration might have seemed excusable. The sun of all his golden hopes had set into a sea of mud. The age of Vane and Hampden had been succeeded by the age of Tom Chiffinch and Samuel Pepys. I say that under such an earthquake of calamity his very trust in God might have been rudely shaken, and Hope might have dropped her anchor and Faith itself have quenched her star. The afternoon of life is often cloudy for us all. Misfortune, disappointment, sickness, the loss of those we love, crowd upon it, and even after the rain the clouds return. And I have known men and even good men, who, in the ruin of fortune, in the anguish of bereavement, in the roar of unjust obloquy, have lost even their faith in God. But Milton, greatest of all amid the total loss of friends, fortune, fame, sight, and hope, persecuted but not forsaken, cast down but not destroyed, poor yet making many rich, fell back on his own great mind, on his own pure aspirations, on his own undaunted purpose, on his own heroic confidence in God. Even as a youth he had spoken in one of his Italian sonnets of the heart within him, which he had found faithful, intrepid, and secure from vulgar fears and hopes, a heart which armed itself as with solid adamant when thunders burst, and the great world roared around.

"And that heart did not fail him now. The shadows of his blindness and obscurity were to him as the shadow of God's wing, under which he took refuge till the tyranny was overpast. He lived hard by in this parish, in Petty France, now York Street. There you might have seen him—England's blind Mæonides—playing his organ in that lonely room with the faded green hangings, or sitting in his gray coat at the door, and turning to the sunlight wistfully his sightless eyes. In those years it was that he wrote for England her one epic poem, 'Paradise Lost.' He had planned it thirty years before, and he received for it £5. It is not for me to speak of the unequaled grandeur of this poem. It is not addressed to the petty, the sensual, or the sordid. Let all whose souls are ignoble keep aloof from that holy ground. It was not meant for them. Milton never cared for the throng and noises of vulgar men. The eagle does not greatly worry itself about the opinions of the mole. If you do not rise to him, he will not stoop to you.

"And after 'Paradise Lost' he gave us 'Paradise Regained,' one of the earliest attempts since the Gospels really to study the great ideal of the character of Christ. And lastly, he wrote 'Samson Agonistes,' a most true index of his heart. In its pure grace and greatness, in its disdainful rejection of all ornament or color, in the austerity of its Greek-like self-restraint, that great tragedy has been compared to a white marble statue from the hand of Phidias. Yet, like the statue of the dying gladiator, it throbs with a pathos too deep for utterance. It reveals to us, under the agonies of the ignoble Samson, the image of the poet himself, struggling amid the storms of fate, yet ploughing his way to peace amid a cloud of rude detractions. And the poet is even grander than his poem. His was the heroism of a soul which no amount of adversity could quell. He was with Samson

'Eyeless in Gaza at a mill with slaves.'

"This was the characteristic of that great affliction wherewith God afflicted him, that he was *remediless*. In that cloudy afternoon of life of which I spoke, in those paler and less crowned, and more anxious and more painful years which come to most of us, the sun often bursts forth at last and turns the clouds into gold and crimson,

'As he descendeth proudly carpeting
The western waves with glory, ere he deign
To set his foot upon them.'

"It was not so with Milton. He says, in those pathetic words of Samson—

> ' Nor am I in the list of those who hope,
> Hopeless are all my evils.'

"And yet he sang on, did not lay aside his laurel; he sang the immortal strains of ' Paradise Lost,'

> ' With voice unchanged
> To hoarse or mute, tho' fall'n on evil days,
> On evil days tho' fall'n, and evil tongues,
> In darkness, and with dangers compassed round
> And solitude.'

And, amid these complicated trials, he says :—

> ' I argue not
> Against heaven's will, but still bear up and steer
> Uphillward.'

"His 'Samson Agonistes' has been called 'the thundering reverberation of a mighty spirit struck with the plectrum of disappointment.' Disheartened, dishonored, yet he was so undismayed that he could still, like Dante in his bitter exile, give to England poems monumental, and imperishable in their splendor and stateliness, which will endure while time shall last. Whatever then may have been Milton's errors, yet if it be noble to be in boyhood earnest and diligent, in youth temperate, serious, and pure ; if there be grandeur in that concentrated and life-long purpose which **St. Paul** describes by '**This** one thing I do;'—if there be anything fruitful in the self-sacrifice which **is** ready, at the call of seeming duty, to lay aside without a murmur the highest hopes;—if there be anything excellent in whole-hearted sincerity, shown **in a** chaste **and** laborious life—if **it be heroic to bow** with unmurmuring submission to the sternest dispen**sations** of Providence; if it be noble to maintain the undauntedness of an upright manhood, and to render to thankless generations immortal services amid the roar of unscrupulous execration, then surely we **may** learn lessons from this life of intent labor, **exalted** aims, and stainless chastity, of a fortitude which never swerved, and **a** duty **which** never succumbed to weariness.

"When Milton had nothing to look forward to **on** earth, save death, as the close and balm of all his sufferings, yet never for one moment did he doubt whether God or Dagon was the Lord. **And** he had this reward of all his undaunted faithfulness, that when man forsook him God was still with him, and, like Athanasius, he had two sure friends. For may we not say of him, as Hooker has said of Athanasius, that there was nothing observed in him throughout the course of that long tragedy other than such as very well became a wise man to do, and a righteous to suffer? so that this was the plain condition of those times, the whole world against him, and he against it; half a hundred years spent in doubtful trial which of the two in the end would prevail, the side which had all, or else the poet which had no friend but God and death—the one a defender of his innocency, the other a finisher of all his troubles.

"Let me conclude with the fine tribute to Milton of a kindred spirit, Wordsworth. The sweet Poet of the Lakes was as ardent a royalist, as earnest a conservative as any one here present could possibly be, and he was, moreover, an eminently holy man. Yet he knew the preciousness to every nation of high examples, and he does not hesitate to say:—

> ' Milton, thou shouldst be living at this hour.
>   England hath need of thee! She is a fen
>   Of stagnant waters. Altar, sword, and pen,
> Fireside, the heroic wealth of hall and bower
>   Are passing from us, we are selfish men.
>   O raise us up, return to us again,
> And give us manners, freedom, virtue, power.
> Thy soul was like a star, and dwelt apart,
>   Thou hadst a voice whose sound was like the sea,
>   Pure as the naked heavens, majestic, free,
>   So didst thou travel on life's common way
> In cheerful godliness—and yet thy heart
>   The lowliest burdens on itse'f did lay.'

" And since high and holy lives are none so common, let us thank God for this and every example of those who, with whatever failures, have yet striven from childhood to old age to walk in the steps of their Saviour Christ."

The foregoing sermon was published in 'The Churchman,' of New York, and to it was appended the following note :—

"St. Margaret's, Westminster,
"February 19, 1888.

"This manuscript of a sermon preached at St. Margaret's, Westminster—the Church of the House of Commons—on the occasion of the unveiling of the Window in memory of Milton, presented to the church by George W. Childs, Esq., of Philadelphia, is presented to Mr. Childs, with grateful regard, by

"FREDERICK W. FARRAR,
"Archdeacon of Westminster."

The subjoined editorial reference to the Window was printed in the same number of 'The Churchman':

"Under the shadow almost of the northern transept of Westminster Abbey and within a stone's throw of Westminster Hall and the Houses of Parliament stands a church which is probably known to every American who has visited London—the Church of St. Margaret's. Interesting as it is because of its monuments and its being the Church of the House of Commons, it has just now gained an added attraction in the Memorial Window to Milton, which has been placed there by the munificence of Mr. George W. Childs, of Philadelphia."

AMERICAN COMMENT.

The leading newspapers of the United States very generally published interesting accounts by cable of the dedicatory ceremonies, with appropriate comments thereupon. From the mass of such accounts or comments which were collected by the Editor he has selected the following only from the 'Brooklyn Eagle' of February 19, 1888, as suggestive of the character of them all:—

"Yesterday the ceremony of unveiling the Milton Memorial Window presented to St. Margaret's Church, Westminster, by George W. Childs, Esq., of Philadelphia, attracted one of the largest congregations ever gathered within the walls of the venerable edifice. Archdeacon Farrar preached the sermon, postponing his usual Lenten exhortation and confining his remarks to the lessons of Christianity as exemplified by the noble life of the great English poet and moralist. The brief extracts communicated by cable indicate that the effort was worthy of the speaker and the occasion. He confessed the satisfaction it gave him that the Church of St. Margaret's should furnish another illustration of those bonds of common blood, traditions, language, and affection which unite the mother country with her marvelous offspring, the giant Republic of the West, and alluded to the peculiar fitness of the honor done by an American to the memory of one who represented much that was most deeply loved in the Commonwealth, which, failing in England, inspired vigor and nobleness in the Commonwealth to which it gave birth beyond the sea.

"Need it be said that the countrymen of Mr. Childs participate with him in the reciprocation of the feeling which inspired these utterances of Archdeacon Farrar? The motive that prompted the Philadelphia philanthropist is a motive which challenges the approval and sympathy of every enlightened American. There is, in his gift of the Milton Window, a teaching larger than that of any sect, class, or faction. **It has** even a nobler significance than that to which the archdeacon adverted. It means more than a recognition of the ties that unite the two leading nations of the Anglo-Saxon race. It is an expression **of** the veneration which fills every elevated mind for one of the **most** extraordinary examples in the history of genius and virtue. In conceiving this honor to the memory of Milton, MR. CHILDS revealed, not only the benevolence of his nature, but his appreciation of the truly great and good. Like **his** Shakspeare Memorial **and the** beautiful Windows in the ancient Abbey that recall the genius of Herbert **and Cowper, it bespeaks the** lofty ideals not less than the kindly **impulses of the donor.**

"**Of** the author of 'Paradise Lost,' it **has** been said **that** he is withdrawn from the ordinary world as an **Alp** is withdrawn—by vastness, by **solitariness of** snows, and by commerce with heaven. MR. CHILDS has shown that the ordinary world may venture **to** invade this **isolation and to** mitigate the grandeur **of** the **poet's solitude by the proofs** that his genius cannot thus divorce him from the great heart of humanity. If the sublimity of his intellect **and** the austerity of his morals lift him far above **his** kind, **the** pathos **of his life and** those passages in which he confesses his heritage of weakness and sorrow, make him our brother and equal. Wisely has Mr. Childs chosen this last object of his generosity and munificence. Fittingly have the English people, speaking by the tongue of Archdeacon Farrar, accepted the offering as at once a tribute to the mighty dead and as a pledge of the fraternity of the race that boasts his ashes as a consecrated legacy."

THE BISHOPS ANDREWES AND KEN MEMORIAL

IN

ST. THOMAS'S CHURCH, WINCHESTER.

THE REREDOS OF ST. THOMAS'S CHURCH, WINCHESTER.

AMONG the gifts which MR. CHILDS has made to England is that of the Reredos which now is one of the most striking adornments of St. Thomas's Church, Winchester.

The inception of this gift is to be found in a letter written October 11, 1887, to MR. CHILDS by his friend, the Reverend Arthur B. Sole, Rector of St. Thomas's Church.

Referring to the Herbert and Cowper Memorial in Westminster Abbey, and to the Shakspeare Fountain at Stratford, Mr. Sole said:—

"Now that you have shown the Midland Counties and the Metropolis an American citizen's appreciation of England's great poets, you must not leave out in the cold the ancient city of the country, Winchester, the one centre to which every American is attracted.

"Could you not give us a monument or memorial to Bishop Ken, who lived close under the shadow of St. Thomas's old Church? We sorely need a new Reredos, and coming from a well-known citizen of that Greater Britain beyond the sea the gift would be highly esteemed by Englishmen."

With this request MR. CHILDS complied with characteristic generosity.

In a letter bearing date December 6, 1887, the Rev. Mr. Sole said: "We feel very grateful to you for your ready compliance with my request, and for choosing our Church as the recipient of your gift which shall show respect and veneration for the good Bishop Ken. The church is a very noble one, and the largest in Winchester, so that it is fitting his monument shall be in it.

"When your gift comes to be told of it is not unlikely that the Cathedral authorities will think that they, perhaps, had the first claim. I think not, however, for the good Bishop was a parish Churchman, and loved to worship in his Churches, only visiting his Cathedral for state and special services.

"It has been suggested that you might like to have good Bishop Andrewes's name connected with Bishop Ken in the work, since he was very often with us in Winchester, and the Church of the seventeenth century owes much to him."

On December 10, 1888, the Rector of St. Thomas's again wrote to MR. CHILDS to acknowledge a draft for a sum sufficient to pay for the execution of the work. He said: "We all feel very grateful to you for your keen interest in St. Thomas's Church which your generous draft so substantially expresses.

"I waited, before acknowledging it, until I could inclose a rough sketch of the design.

"I have made known your kind response to my suggestion to the Dean and the Bishop, and they were in accord that your gift manifests a most fraternal feeling for the OLD MOTHER COUNTRY which is most pleasing to us. They agreed with me that it would be most fitting, if the gift should take the form of a carved stone Reredos for the Church. In your kind letter you said: 'I leave the money in your hands to do with it as you deem best.'

"We thought of a Window and drew out plans.

"The positions in the East where we should like to have placed it are already filled, and as the windows are large we thought the Reredos might manifest and demonstrate portions of 'the Te Deum' very suitably, so as to carry out your wish to commemorate Bishop Ken and Bishop Andrewes.

"The Church is dedicated to St. Thomas and St. Clement, so we are grouping *them* in one panel, and opposite to them Bishop Ken and Bishop Andrewes. This enables us to insert the words below this group, so helpful and appropriate since the gift comes from across the seas, 'The Holy Church throughout all the world doth acknowledge Thee.'

"The stone masons will be at work upon the Reredos in a yard just opposite the place where Bishop Ken's house was situate, and in the garden of the palace in which Bishop Andrewes lived."

Again, on December 28, 1888, the Rev. Mr. Sole wrote to Mr. Childs, saying :—

"The following resolution was passed at a special and influential Vestry that was called last week to discuss the Reredos:—

"' Parish of St. Thomas and St. Clement,
Winchester.

"'At a Vestry meeting held according to due notice on Thursday, the 20th day of December, 1888, to consider the subject of the gift of a Reredos to the Church by an American citizen, and to record a vote of thanks to the donor :—

"'Proposed by Captain Budden and seconded by Mr. Alfred King, that this meeting of the Rector, Church-wardens, and parishioners in Vestry assembled, do hereby offer to GEORGE WILLIAM CHILDS, Esquire, of Philadelphia, U. S. A., their most cordial thanks for his very handsome gift towards the beautifying of their parish Church, and to which they would beg to add the hope that, should MR. CHILDS ever visit England, they may have the pleasure of seeing him in Winchester, and thanking him in person for the kindly interest he has shown in this ancient city and parish of the Old Mother Country.

"'ALFRED KING,
"'J. A. MORRAH (Colonel),
"'Church Wardens.
"'ARTHUR N. SOLE, Rector.'

"The Reredos is now progressing in the workmen's hands, and I hope to be able soon to send you a photograph of it in its completed state."

On February 15, 1889, the Rector of St. Thomas's wrote to MR. CHILDS as follows regarding the Memorial:—

"The Reredos is growing rapidly, and will be unveiled at 4.30 on Friday afternoon, March 1, by the Very Reverend, the Dean of Worcester.

"He is a most eloquent preacher, and I have no doubt will say some helpful words concerning the circumstances under which the erection is made, and your very sympathetic kindness and good-will toward the old city of your Fathers.

'The inscription I have not yet prepared. I have waited to take counsel with the Bishop. I should like it to take such a form as this:—

'To the glory of God, this Reredos has been erected by GEORGE W. CHILDS, of Philadelphia, U. S. A., and to record the undying esteem that is shared by the Church of the New World, reciprocally with the ancient city of Winchester, in the saintly lives of two of her sons and citizens, Bishop Andrewes and Bishop Ken.'

"The Reredos was unveiled last Friday before a large concourse of worshipers. It looked very beautiful, and was spoken of by many as a munificent gift of love from you.

"We all recognize it as a work expressive of your sympathy and intercommunion of spirit with us, as you co-operate to promote the beauty and reverence of God's sanctuary in this ancient city.

"I hope you will like the inscription that we have placed upon it. The wording of it is that of Canon Basil Wilberforce. We shall all much hope, some day, to see you in Winchester, that we may show you our church, the ripening outward beauty of which, I pray God, is but correspondent to the inward progression of souls spiritually built up within it."

AN ACCOUNT OF THE DEDICATION.

Under the caption of "The New Reredos at St. Thomas's, Winchester," 'The Hampshire Gazette,' in its issue of March 2, 1889, of that ancient metropolis said:—

"An interesting and historical Reredos has been placed in the Church of Sts. Thomas and Clement, Winchester, under unusually pleasing circumstances, connecting Old and New England. A friend of the Rector's (the Rev. A. B. Sole), Mr. Childs, of Philadelphia, presented him with a check to defray the cost of a Reredos to commemorate Bishops Lancelot Andrewes and Ken, prelates certainly of saintly renown, whose names and fame are revered wherever Englishmen are, for both were staunch Churchmen; both have left writings which are yet prized as manuals of devotion and aids to religion; and both have an historic interest, for Andrewes administered the Diocese of Canterbury whilst the Primate from an accident to his keeper was held to be incapacitated, and Ken was one of the 'Seven Bishops.' Both are to be remembered for their learning, and Ken especially to be honored for his firmness of purpose against William III. (when Prince of Orange), Charles II., and James, when he considered morality and honor were jeopardized. Of Andrewes it may be said his preaching was excellent, and James I., who in Presbyterian Scotland always had some doubts about the sermon in prospect, in England was delighted with Andrewes as a preacher. Ken rebuked here, when he was a prebend, Charles II.; and he is honored also as a Wykehamist. It is pleasant to know that Charles, although Ken refused his house for the use of Nell Gwynne, respected the 'little man,' and made him Bishop of Bath and Wells. The Reredos is a very handsome work, although it includes the arcade of the former one, which consisted of panels with the Commandments, etc. These are now removed to another place close by, and the spandrils of the arches have been carved with conventional foliage and fruit, and an angel in the north and south spandrils. Above this arcade is another of five panels, forming, with its cornice and cross, a pediment or finish to the Reredos. The cross, with the *Agnus Dei* painted in colors, surmounts the whole, and the hand-mouldings and

other ornaments of the shafts of the panels are in the best style of work. The stonework is from a design by Mr. Herbert Kitchin, and is of early English character. Caen stone has been used. The carvings have been very beautifully executed by Mr. A. Whitley, the carver from the Cathedral, under the supervision of Mr. B. T. Kitchin. The stonework of the Reredos was by the Cathedral staff of masons, under their foreman, Mr. Hodges. In the panels are fixed as many paintings by ladies of Winchester. In the centre is Christ ascending and blessing; on either side are angels with the chalice and 'golden crown;' and on the outer panels are, on the south, Saints Thomas, the apostle, and Clement, the third Bishop of Rome, martyred in the time of Trajan, each with emblems—the spear and the anchor; in the north are representations of Andrewes standing with his pastoral staff, and Ken kneeling, both vested in Reformation robes, and with mitres at their feet. The pastoral staff indicates that Andrewes died in office, whereas Ken, from scruples of conscience, died out of office, being a non-juror. Close to this panel is another in the wall over the credence table, which bears, under a cross-surmounted globe delineating England and America, the following words—
'*Stat Crux dum evolvit orbis*,' followed by this inscription:—

'In token of the unity of spirit and bond of peace between the Churches of the Old and New World, this Reredos is dedicated by GEORGE W. CHILDS, of Philadelphia, to the memory of two Bishops of the Church universal, both connected with this Cathedral city— Bishop Lancelot Andrewes and Bishop Ken.—MDCCCLXXXIX.'

The lower panels have also paintings of angels with musical instruments typical of praise. These, like the upper tier, are by Winchester ladies, and it is not flattering to say that their work is artistic, striking, and well worthy of the place, the Church, and the prelates commemorated by this liberal Trans-Atlantic Churchman and lover of the Mother Country, from which he is proud to trace his family: and whilst we allude to descent, let it not be forgotten that the family of Lancelot Andrewes is extant in the person of the worthy Master of St. Cross, and also, we believe, in that of the Rev. Dr. Fearon. Mr. Jelly, of this city, has executed some of the color decorations essential to the design. The arcade, in addition to the Reredos, which runs across the east end of the church, has been renovated and carved.

"The Reredos was unveiled yesterday (St. David's Day), at Choral Evensong. There was a numerous congregation. The service opened with the Old Hundredth Psalm. The anthem was 'How amiable are Thy tabernacles,' and it was well sung by the choir. The hymn before the sermon was 'We love the place, O God.' The preacher was the Very Rev. Dr. Gott, Dean of Worcester, who chose for his text the words 'From strength to strength,' from the seventh verse of the 84th Psalm. In the course of an eloquent sermon he said they were met together that afternoon to worship God, not only in spirit but in truth, and to give a blessing in God's name to the new addition to the altar which graced their church, and indicated their devotion. Their church was dedicated in a twofold way to St. Thomas and St. Clement. The city of Winchester was dear to him as one who owed to the School of Winchester all the little learning that he had. A great living writer had said 'History is our modern prophecy.' The history we could recall to-day, which was personified in names so well known as St. Thomas, St. Clement, Bishop Andrewes, and Bishop Ken, was prophecy at this end of the nineteenth century. Professor Westcott when he used these words meant that what had been done once might be done again. But he meant more than this; he meant that God is the same yesterday, to-day, and for ever, and that what God did for the men whose names were bound up with that church and their city He was ready to do even for them and him. Yes, he meant that the history of the past had gone on increasing in its power, in its beauty, in its holiness. Its motto had been 'From strength to strength.' From age to age we had been ascending higher and nearer to God, and in these last days there arose before the hearts of those who strove to see God a giddy height on which we were standing, a very pinnacle of the Temple, on which, if we were no better than our fathers, we were far worse. In these days we might see more of the power of God than in the martyr days. As the coming of God drew nearer the Church must be more prepared. The Church was riper, the long summer-time had done its work, and the golden age of the Christendom of God was not the beginning of the Church, but its more splendid close—that close which perhaps it was destined he and they should see and take part in. As they looked across the ages to Clement and his fellow-Christians in St. Paul's time, and compared the conditions under which they worshiped with the freedom of the present day, it was indeed a great step from strength to strength. Coming to the others of the group of figures, the Dean said it might be there existed the thought that as the worshipers looked on those portraits of Bishop Andrewes and Bishop Ken they might be stimulated to pray as they did—fervently, purely, trusting in Christ by the help of the Holy

Ghost. The preacher passed in brief review the distinguishing features in the lives and characters of Bishop Andrewes and Bishop Ken—Andrewes the great lover of boys, the great lover of nature, the man greatly beloved, the great lover of God; Ken the Winchester schoolboy, the Wykehamist, the mention of whose name touched a chord which vibrated in more hearts than his in the church; Ken who at the bidding of conscience gave up liberty, possessions, and what was more precious than all, his pastoral work; Ken who so honored his King that in spite of what happened he gave up all rather than express allegiance to the man he regarded as an usurper when that king was a fugitive and an outcast. Concluding, he asked what was the strength added to their Church since the days of Ken? He did not think he could put it in words—he could not hold the world in his hands, he could not express the mighty strength which had come over the Church of God from those days till now! How wide the Church had spread, how fertile had been her daughter Churches within the last century, how rich she was in founding new branches of the old Church, how strong in infusing the spirit of the one true religion—the religion of Christ—into the old religions of the East! How wonderful had been the strength of the Church in the country of the donor who sent the offering to the city whence these two saintly men came! Were they personally going from strength to strength? As years passed over them, and as the troubles—perhaps the pleasures—of life thickened around them, were they going from strength to strength? Let the faith be handed on pure and untarnished to their children, and their children's children, until at last they appeared before Him who was their Almighty strength, and more than conquerors received from Him the power which Eternity would bring. The hymn 'Lift the strain of high thanksgiving' was sung during the offertory."

The Story of MR. CHILDS's Memorials to some of the noblest of Old England's worthies, which is here brought to an end, has grown under the hands of the Editor, despite his efforts to keep it within modest limits. But long as it is, he indulges, at least, the hope that it will be found interesting to those who agree with him that it is permitted to no one to do better work in this world than that of fostering fraternal feeling between peoples who are akin, but who are separated by the broad ocean, and who have been sometimes estranged by misunderstandings, conflicting interests, or untoward circumstances.

This is the work which Mr. Childs appears to the Editor to have had a mind to do in the making of every one of those memorial gifts to our cousins across the sea with whom Americans can claim even a closer degree of consanguinity than that of cousinship— their just claim is that of Common Brotherhood.

The sacred poets, Herbert and Cowper; Milton, the sublime singer of the Cromwellian epoch; and Shakspeare, whose genius illuminates the present not less effulgently than it glorified the age of Elizabeth, spoke, and still do speak, in no strange tongue, but in our very own, in that of our Mother Country. In these great Masters of the English language, in their work and in their fame, Americans have also their full share and part, and whoso gives recognition to that which they did and reverence to their memories in noble, impressive monuments does that which strengthens the feeling of fraternity which nature itself demands should exist between the two countries, whose peoples are of the same blood, and the fame of whose men of noble thought and deed is their common heritage. This, as it seems to the Editor, is what Mr. Childs has done, and for doing which he deserves the warmest gratitude of England and America.

INDEX.

AMERICANS, Matthew Arnold's criticism of, 196–198.
Anderson, Mary, 146.
Andrewes, Lancelot, Bishop, 242–243, 244, 247–248, 253.
Annesley, Rev. F. H., 50.
Arbuthnot, Rev. G., 50.
Arden, Mary, mother of Shakspeare, 23, 147.
ARNOLD, SIR EDWIN, 88; editorial of, 89–96.
ARNOLD, MATTHEW, 194; address of, 196–205; death of, 205.

BACON, DELIA, theory of, 28.
Baltimore 'Daily News,' extract from, 142–144.
Barnard, Rev. W., 50.
Barnum, P. T., proposal of, to remove Shakspeare's house to America, 64, 111, 145.
Basse's 'Elegy on Shakspeare,' 3.
Bird, Alderman of Stratford, 15, 33, 50, 153.
Birmingham 'Daily Post,' extract from, 107–115.

BISHOPS ANDREWES AND KEN MEMORIAL, in St. Thomas's Church, Winchester, 241–255.
Booth, Edwin, 145, 146.
Bright, John, quotation from, 156.
Brooklyn 'Eagle,' extracts from, 23–30, 235–238.

CHILDS, GEORGE W., letter from, 190; letter to, extracts from, 177; telegram from, 78; water from Fountain sent to, 107, 129.
Coleridge, Samuel Taylor, 29.
Cook, Joel, 179.
Cossins, J. A., architect of Fountain, 17, 50, 104.
Cowper, William, 173–174, 176.

DEDICATION OF FOUNtain, Account of, 30–34, 106–107, 126–130.
De La Warr, Earl, 33, 49, 82, 87, 117, 126; he proposes toast to President of United States, 52.
Description of Fountain, 17–18, 19–21, 108–109, 150–151.
Dilke, Sir Chas. Wentworth, 168.

Index

EMERSON, RALPH WALdo, quotation from, 73.
'Evening Wisconsin,' Milwaukee, extract from, 139-141.

FARRAR, F. W., D. D., Archdeacon of Westminster, letters from, 188-190, 191-195; quotations from, 169-171, 187; sermon by, 212-234, 236.
Field, Kate, 146.
Flower, Charles E., 16, 33, 49, 84, 145, 153; he proposes toast to Mr. Henry Irving, 70-72.
Flower, Edgar, 33, 50, 84, 153.

GARRICK, DAVID, portrait of, by Gainsborough, 130, 147; quotation from, 2.
Gott, Rev. Dr., Dean of Worcester, sermon by, 251-254.
Gower, Lord Ronald, 50, 82, 88, 97, 117, 124.
Grant, Baron, erects statue to Shakspeare, 3.

HALLIWELL-PHILLIPPS, James O., 1, 35.
'Hampshire Gazette,' extract from, 247-254.
'Harper's Magazine,' extract from, 187.
'Harper's Weekly,' extract from, 144-156.

Hathaway, Anne, 85, 90, 100, Hall, Hon. A. Oakey, 125.
HERBERT AND COWPER MEMORIAL in Westminster Abbey, 161-179.
Herbert, George, quotation from Walton's life of, 172-173.
'Historical Memorials,' quotations from, 161-163.
HODGSON, SIR ARTHUR, Mayor of Stratford, 11, 12, 15, 16, 17, 32, 33, 38, 76-77, 82, 83, 87, 97, 103, 106, 108, 116-117, 122, 126, 149; proposes toasts to Queen and the rest of the Royal Family, 51-52; receives message of thanks from Mr. Childs, 78.
HOLMES, OLIVER W., poet, letter from, 22; poem of, 41-44, 106, 110, 113, 129, 134, 137, 141.

IRVING, HENRY, 31, 32, 33, 34, 40, 82, 84, 88, 91, 92, 93, 94, 96, 97, 98, 99, 102, 103, 106, 107, 108, 110, 113, 114, 117, 118, 119, 122, 124, 134, 137, 138, 143; drinks to Shakspeare in first water that flows from Fountain, 49; reads Mr. Holmes's poem, 41; responds to Mr. Flower's toast, 72-75; speech of, 44-48, 127-129, 131, 141.
Irving, Washington, 29, 36, 80, 87, 109, 114, 134, 145.

'Illustrated London News,' extract from, 16–17.

JONSON, BEN, 2, 3, 4, 24, 25.

KEN, THOMAS, BISHOP, 242, 244, 247–248, 253.
Kitchin, Herbert, designer of reredos, 249.

LAFFAN, REV. R. S. DE C., 50, 88.
Laffan, Mrs. R. S. de C., poem by, 78–79.
Liverpool 'Post,' extract from, 115–120.
London 'Daily Telegraph,' extract from, 83–87.
London Globe,' extract from, 97–98.
London 'Standard,' extract from, 99–102.
London 'Times,' extracts from, 13, 79–82.
LOWELL, JAMES RUSSELL, letter from, 35–38, 88, 94, 98, 99, 101, 103, 106, 110, 113, 114, 119, 134, 137, 138, 141; lines of, under Sir Walter Raleigh Window, 189.

MACAULAY, JAMES, M. D., 9, 10, 11, 12, 13, 16, 17, 39, 40, 50, 82, 83, 88, 103, 107, 117, 126, 129, 131;

his response to toast to Mr. Childs, 69–70.
Marshall, Frank, 51, 85.
Martin, Sir Theodore, K. C. B., 50, 82, 88, 106, 117, 124, 126; he proposes toast to Shakspeare, 60–62, 83.
Milton, John, 184, 186, 187, 188–189, 199–205, 255; encomium of, 216–233.
MILTON WINDOW in St. Margaret's Church, Westminster, 183–238.

NEW YORK 'HERALD,' extracts from, 13–15, 17–18, 125–132.
New York 'Times,' extracts from, 136–137.
New York 'World,' extracts from, 19–21, 120–124.
New York 'Commercial Advertiser,' extract from, 137–139.
Nevin, W. W., 178.

OWEN, SIR PHILIP CUNliffe, 50, 82, 88, 97, 103, 117, 124, 126; remarks of, 48, 98, 131.

'PALL MALL GAZETTE,' extract from, 102–107.
'Paradise Lost,' Milton's, 229.
'Paradise Regained,' Milton's, 229.
Parkinson, J. C, 51, 85, 88, 117.

Index.

Pew in St. Margaret's, appropriated to Americans, 186, 214.
PHELPS, HON. EDWARD J., American Minister to England, 33, 40, 45, 49, 82, 83, 87, 94, 95, 97, 103, 106, 111, 117, **119**, 124, 126, 127, 131, 134, **137**, 193, **211**; his response to toast to President of United States, **53-59.**
Philadelphia 'Evening Telegraph,' extract from, 133-134.
Philadelphia 'Public Ledger,' extract from, **166-167.**
Philadelphia 'Times,' extract from, 135.
PRESIDENT OF UNITED STATES, toast to, **52.**

RALEIGH, SIR WALTER, Memorial Window to, in St. Margaret's, 187, 189, 213.
Red Horse Inn, 147
Resolution of Council of Stratford, accepting Fountain, **12, 13.**
Resolution of thanks to Mr. Childs, from Vestry of St. Thomas's Church, 245.

ST. MARGARET'S CHURCH Westminster, origin of, 185; Milton Window in, 10, 149, 183-238; description of, 194, 207-208; unveiling of, 193-194, **235-236**; pew in for Americans, 186, 214; Raleigh window in, 187, 189, 213.
St. Thomas's Church, Winchester, reredos in, 241, 243-244, 245, 247; description of, 248-250; unveiling of, 250-251.
Sala, George Augustus, 16.
'Samson Agonistes,' Milton's, 230-231.
Shakspeare, John, father of Shakspeare, 1, 26, 90.
Shakspeare, Richard, ancestor of Shakspeare, 1.
Shakspeare, William, 1, **2, 3, 4, 5, 10,** 23, 24, 25, **26,** 28, 29, **46-47, 60-62, 72-73,** 89-91, **100-101, 102, 111, 142,** 201, 220, 255; pall-bearer of, **29**; toast to, **60-62.**
Shakspeare Inn, 147.
Shakspeare Memorial Building, 86, **145.**
Site of Fountain selected, 16-17.
Sole, Rev. Arthur B., letters from, 241-247.
STANLEY, REV. ARTHUR P., Dean of Westminster, **15, 39,** 109, 161-167, 177, 178; letters from, 6-7, 7-8; note by, 175-176.
"State Services" in St. Margaret's Church, 186.
STRATFORD-UPON-AVON FOUNTAIN, 1-157.
Stratford-upon-Avon 'Herald,' extract from, 30-79.
'Sunday at Home,' London, extract from, 175-176.

Index.

TIMMINS, SAMUEL, 13, 16, 51, 85, 88, 111; he proposes toast to Sir Arthur Hodgson, 75-77.

Trinity Holy Church, Stratford, 100, 146; effigy of Shakspeare in, 2; memorial window proposed for, 6, 7-8; proposed restoration of, 9.

VICTORIA, QUEEN, Jubilee Year of, 10, 12, 13, 15, 16, 17, 19, 31, 39, 44, 57, 92; message from, 59, 95, 98, 99, 110, 115, 119, 122; toast to, 51-52.

'Vignettes of Travel,' quotation from, 178-179.

WALTER, JOHN, proprietor London 'Times,' 50, 82, 87, 88, 97, 105, 110, 114, 117, 126, 131-132; proposes toast to Mr. Childs and gives short sketch of his life, 62-68.

Walton, Izaak, 172.

Warwick 'Advertiser,' extract from, 99.

Westminster Abbey, 161-172, 177; bust of Shakspeare in, 2, 3; Herbert and Cowper Memorial Window in, 6, 10, 15, 17, 27, 39, 97, 109, 116, 148, 165-167; description of, 176.

WHITTIER, JOHN G., letters from, 38, 110, 113, 209; lines by, 208, 216.

Williams, Roger, 215.

Winter, William, 144.

Woodcock, Catherine, wife of Milton, 186, 187, 195, 199.

Wordsworth, William, quotations from, 217, 219, 233.

www.ingramcontent.com/pod-product-compliance
Lightning Source LLC
Chambersburg PA
CBHW032002230426
43672CB00010B/2242